Freight Broker Business Startup

How to Start a Freight Brokerage Company and Go from Business Plan to Marketing and Scaling

Table of Contents

Introduction
Chapter 1: The Freight Brokerage Industry
Chapter 2: Why Become a Freight Broker
Chapter 3: Building Your Empire
Chapter 4: Adapt or Perish
Chapter 5: Pricing and Competition
Chapter 6: All about Business Plans
Chapter 7: The Cost of Starting Up
Chapter 8: Can I Work from Home?
Chapter 9: Scaling Your Business
Chapter 10: Staffing, Money Management and Crises
Conclusionì

Introduction

Are you working in the trucking business and want to find a new way to increase your income? This book shows you the ins and outs of the freight brokerage industry and how to become a successful freight broker. Don't worry; this book covers everything you need to know about the industry, even if you've never heard of the term.

Many people are looking for ways to have a complementary job that they could develop into a full-time job as business owners. Freight brokerage has been a growing industry because of the high demand for brokers in the market. With the current conditions due to the COVID pandemic, many people are looking for ways to establish a company remotely and with minimum costs.

This book will provide an overview of the industry and how it has gained popularity over time. The technological advancements have made this industry an attractive choice for many people to shift their careers to becoming freight brokers. You will learn the different types of freight agents and the most common reasons you should become a freight broker.

This book contains easy-to-follow guidelines on how to get started in the industry. You will learn about all the paperwork needed to register your company. This book outlines the qualities and skills required to become a freight broker. By following the various tips and tricks described throughout the book, you will have the perfect guide with you to take the leap and become your own boss.

You will learn the importance of technology and digitalization in this industry. Since you are looking to work from home, communication is key. You will learn how to use marketing strategies and techniques that are guaranteed to get you noticed in the market. You will discover how to stand out among your competitors without changing all the game's rules.

If you want to be a serious competitor in this business, you need competitive rates. These will play a significant role in establishing relationships with new clients. This book will show you how to calculate an estimated rate as your commission to deliver shipments. You will learn how to spot your competition and perform analyses used by the biggest companies in the business, not just locally but also globally.

You will find methods to outline your business plan and turn it into reality. This book contains various tips and tricks and recommended courses to help you improve your skills. You will find out what it takes to start a company from home and how you can sustain your business. Discover how to scale your business and track your progress, or even adjust your business plan as needed to upgrade your business transactions. Let's dive into the world of freight brokerage and learn how to target a specific niche in the market and how that can positively impact your freight brokerage company.

Chapter 1: The Freight Brokerage Industry

Freight brokerage has been around for a long time, but it hasn't always looked the same. In fact, freight brokers have gone through many transformations over the years to keep up with the ever-changing industry. Freight brokerage is an industry that can be confusing to newcomers and veterans alike because of the various roles in play. This chapter will give you an overview of what freight brokerage is all about, how it has evolved over time, and how technology has played a role in its growth.

What Is the Freight Brokerage Business?

Freight brokerage is a type of third-party logistics business. It works as an intermediary process between shippers and carriers to help facilitate the transportation process, but many people find it difficult to understand what exactly goes on behind closed doors in this industry. Freight brokers are responsible for placing loads with carriers that match their customers' needs. This can mean different things for different people, but it generally means breaking down the load into smaller sections so multiple truckers can deliver them on time and intact.

Ideally, freight brokerage would match truckers with shippers, but it's much more complicated than that. The world of freight is complex and ever-changing because there are so many factors to consider when looking for quality carriers that can meet your needs. This has led to brokers specializing in specific areas or regions because they have the expertise required to make these matches.

Brokers also purchase and sell loads to drivers, but they don't actually own the trucks or directly employ any of these people. Instead, brokers work as liaisons between truckers and shippers by receiving the freight from one party and delivering it to another, so there is no interruption in service. This way, customers can focus on their core competencies while relying on brokers to handle their logistics.

What Are the Different Roles in Freight Brokerage?

Freight brokerage is an interesting business because it has different roles for specific responsibilities. Other third-party logistics businesses, like trucking companies or warehouse operators, don't have as many moving parts since they're not responsible for finding carriers to transport their freight. The four main roles in freight brokerage are:

- **Brokers** - The ones who actually find truckers to do the transporting. Depending on their agreements with carriers and shippers, they get paid either commission or a flat rate.

- **Salespeople** – These people work closely with brokers because they're responsible for finding loads that match a carrier's capabilities. They work out the details with shippers and present their options to brokers who find a carrier that will complete the task in time.

- **Field Agents** – These are representatives who check carriers' equipment before, during, and after transport through audits or inspections. Some companies also hire these people for load-planning purposes or scheduling.

- **Dispatchers** – Dispatchers send truckers on their way and then communicate with brokers on the status of a shipment as it makes its way from point A to B. As transportation managers, they're responsible for keeping trucks stocked with materials so drivers can complete deliveries within a reasonable time frame.

Why Do Businesses Need Freight Brokers?

As the online market expands, many businesses realize the need for freight brokers to assist them in moving products. However, some people still think a freight broker is just another middleman and wonder why companies need to hire one when so many logistics providers exist. The following are some of the ways freight brokers can help companies:

- Companies need to be able to move their products around the world. That means working with several different types of carriers, many of which are not direct providers. Freight brokers help companies find these options and work out deals that save them money without sacrificing quality service.

- Freight brokers are experts on the intricacies of freight shipping. They know how to save companies time and money by using less expensive but still high-quality providers.

- Freight brokers keep track of all documents, tariffs, laws, and regulations, etc., so that they can help their clients navigate any changes in the market quickly and easily.

- Freight brokers help companies make the most of their budget by identifying what they genuinely require for moving products rather than just throwing in unnecessary fees.

- Many freight carriers have a minimum size, weight, or other requirements that deter smaller businesses from using them. This means that those businesses cannot work with certain providers. However, a freight broker can negotiate a deal that works for both the business and its carrier.

- There are different types of freight carriers, which means that companies need someone who knows all about them to help figure out which type is best suited for each situation.

- The logistics industry changes quickly, so it's essential for businesses to have someone who can keep up with the changes and help them figure out how to use new developments in their favor. This helps companies stay up-to-date on all changes that affect their supply chains.

The Evolution of the Freight Brokerage Industry

Throughout history, the freight brokerage industry has evolved in response to the needs of shippers.

The earliest years of freight shipping began with the Industrial Revolution in the 1760s. This revolution was when the world was first introduced to high-speed, large-scale, and long-distance transportation. The railroad systems began to monopolize the freight industry in 1820.

The freight brokerage industry did not take shape until the Motor Carrier Act of 1935. New laws and regulations for commercial vehicle drivers were implemented, and motor carriers began to thrive. Regulations were established for the freight industry as drivers, carriers, and brokers were required to obtain licenses. This marked the beginning of a new era for the freight brokerage industry, which started building standards and procedures still in use today.

By the 1950s, nearly 170 billion ton-miles of freight were being transported. The Interstate Highway System was established in 1956, paving the way for about forty thousand miles of highway construction in the United States alone.

The freight brokerage industry consolidated rapidly in the 1970s and 1980s due to larger fleets and an increasing number of brokers entering the industry.

Another significant change occurred in the industry during the 1990s. The trucking industry was deregulated, allowing over half a million independent motor carriers to operate in the United States. By this time, most transportation-management companies had begun to use computers and software, resulting in new standards for brokerage operations that are still in use today.

By the turn of the century, internet technologies were being used to connect brokers with carriers, putting control back in the hands of shippers.

Modern-Day Freight Brokerage

Modern-day freight brokerage is an integral part of the logistics industry. The freight brokerage industry has experienced tremendous change due to automation and digitization. While many industries are still struggling with technology integration, the logistics industry is far ahead, making it easier for brokers to complete their tasks and stay updated on relevant information. Electronic devices enable brokers to quickly access information about their carriers, updates on new regulations, and other important items. With the integration of advanced technologies in freight brokerage operations, companies can take advantage of software that can track all aspects of a shipment from pick-up to delivery. This makes life easier for people involved in logistics management.
Customer service has always been a priority in the freight brokerage industry. With increased access to information, brokers can provide better service at lower costs, causing many companies to abandon traditional shipping methods in favor of third-party logistics providers.

The Last Mile: Focus on Instant Delivery

Ecommerce has dramatically changed the way people shop. People now buy online and expect their purchases to be delivered instantly, rather than wait days for them to arrive by mail or in-store. This is where logistics comes into play with an industry that has gone through significant changes due to eCommerce growth – freight brokerage.

Typically, a package's journey is divided into three parts: the first mile, the middle mile, and the last mile. The first mile is the shortest distance from a fulfillment center or manufacturing plant to a warehouse. The middle mile connects warehouses with their closest distribution hub. Last but not least, the final leg of your package's journey – from the distribution hub to its destination – is referred to as "the last mile."

This poses a significant challenge to the freight brokerage industry because eCommerce orders necessitate remarkably fast service. For example, Amazon's rise and enhanced logistics capabilities have given online shoppers even fewer reasons to visit physical stores. This means that if an order is not taken care of quickly enough, it may be lost forever or never re-ordered due to the customer's negative experience.

One of the biggest challenges for freight brokers is capacity. Capacity can be defined as the number of orders they can take care of at any given time, and it really depends on several factors like geographical location (whether or not there is a direct connection between supply and demand), number of trucks, the size of warehouses, and much more. To meet this challenge, brokers must strike a balance with their logistics partners in terms of capacity and capability to maintain quality service levels for their customers while maintaining profitability themselves. This is where technology can help with tools that optimize network utilization by leveraging real-time data from partners' systems, allowing freight brokers to find capacity that would otherwise be missed.

Stakeholders of the Freight Brokerage Industry

The main stakeholders in the freight brokerage industry are:

Freight Brokers

They are responsible for ensuring that shipments arrive safely at their destination.

Outsourced Logistics Providers (OLP)

The go-between connecting brokers with carriers can be trucking companies or any other type of carrier required.

Warehouse Owners and Operators

They are in charge of warehousing products and making them available to the appropriate carriers at the right time to make deliveries as quickly as possible.

Carriers

The ones actually driving trucks, trains, ships, or airplanes from one place to another. They are a crucial component of any supply chain, so they come at a high cost.

Customers

These are the people for whom freight brokers ultimately work. Their customers are typically online retailers who need to deliver their products quickly and cost-effectively.

Step-By-Step Journey of a Package

The journey of a package typically goes through the following steps:

Tender of the Order

The customer submits their order to the freight broker, who then checks where it needs to be sent and makes sure that a carrier is assigned. The freight broker will also collect information like weight, dimensions, and other special requirements.

Pre-Trip Planning

The broker then works with the carrier to schedule a convenient trip for both parties. This step involves determining if the available carrier(s) can accommodate this particular shipment in terms of size and weight or other restrictions and figuring in variables such as holidays or weather conditions that may affect transport times.

Dispatching the Shipment

When everything is confirmed, the broker sends out a terms document to both parties involved to verify their acceptance of these terms. This "waybill" includes information about the shipment and its final destination and can be accessed through any handheld device with internet access.

Delivery/Collection of Freight

A carrier typically picks up the shipment and takes it to the warehouse, where the broker then gets an update about when the product will be ready for delivery. (A carrier may also pick up a package from one location and drop it off at another, so there is less time for customers' products to go through unnecessary miles or sit idle.)

Arrival of Order at Warehouses

Once an agreement has been reached with a carrier, goods are received from warehouses or manufacturers arranged by the logistics provider. Depending on the nature of the product, it may need to be stored in specific storage locations such as cold storage warehouses.

Delivery to Customers' Address

The final step is to confirm the delivery plan to customers, who can then either sign off on the bill immediately or wait until everything has been confirmed before doing so. The customer can use this information to know when their order will arrive and plan accordingly.

Freight Brokerage Industry Trends

The main trends in the freight brokerage industry are:

- The internet has made it easier for anyone to find a carrier, thanks to online search engines like Google Maps or Transportation Management Systems (TMS), which allow carriers' information to be organized and presented online.

- Big Data allows companies to make better decisions about which carriers they should use for certain shipments and how much it will cost them. Companies can allocate resources more effectively and reduce overall costs by using this information early on – a win-win situation!

- Another trend is the increasingly common use of temperature-controlled trucks. This is a small but critical aspect of logistics that can significantly impact customers' products, especially regarding food safety!

- Another trend in this industry is consolidation from smaller brokerages into larger companies with better resources. This is due to the increasing complexity of freight logistics which has left brokers unable to handle the workload independently.

- The increase in communication between carriers and brokers and customers has allowed all parties to be kept up-to-date on everything going on throughout the process without having to call or email each other individually, saving everyone time.

Companies that want faster deliveries and more reliable services are increasingly outsourcing logistics to save resources and generally lower costs. This is possible with the help of third-party logistics providers (TPLs), who have at their fingertips the scoop on everything from trucks to warehouses and all players in between.

Freight Broker vs. Freight Forwarder vs. Freight Agent

Freight brokers and freight forwarders assist in transporting goods, although they do so via various techniques and specialize in different areas of the freight sector. Freight brokers are mainly interested in the logistics aspect of the industry, as they are responsible for arranging transport between two points.

Freight forwarders frequently provide a variety of services for their clients. These services include warehousing, packaging, combining shipments, filing customs paperwork, etc. Freight forwarders use house bills of lading (HBLs). Freight forwarders frequently operate their own container fleet.

A freight broker will never take possession of the freight. However, a freight forwarder may take possession of the cargo and apply their own HBLs. Freight forwarders are responsible for the cargo's legal liability, including the duty to insure it. In practice, these liability concerns are full of legal grey areas, and freight brokers' responsibility for cargo claims is frequently determined via courts and insurance companies.

At the most basic level, a freight agent is someone (or a group of individuals) who works as independent contractors for a freight broker to transport goods on their behalf. In contrast, the freight broker does it under their own operating license.

A freight agent is unable to pursue every shipment; a freight agent ensures that the potential customer they are dealing with is not already a client of another freight broker agent.

The Future of the Freight Brokerage Industry

An increasing number of companies are turning towards the internet to find carriers for their shipments. This has led to increased demand for freight brokers that understand how the online process works and can help with it.

These brokers will need to create a partnership with their customers, supporting them throughout the shipment process from start to finish, every step of the way.

This implies that they should have access to all types of carrier information, not only price data but also customer reviews, to assist customers in selecting the best carrier for their needs.

This means that brokers will need to create better relationships with carriers hoping to expand their network over time and become more competitive than other companies in this space. These changes mean that freight brokerage is becoming a much bigger industry, which has allowed it to go global as well.

New opportunities are constantly arising in this industry, especially for brokers looking to expand their network of carriers and offer more services than just price quotes.

New entrepreneurs looking to get into the freight brokerage industry should expect tough competition, but they may also expect to be presented with many opportunities. The freight brokerage industry is a billion-dollar business. It has evolved over time, adapting to the needs of its customers and becoming more efficient in this process. Freight brokers are regarded as an intermediary between shippers and carriers; their service assists in transporting goods over long distances by connecting shippers with carriers who can get their products from one location to another for less money. As globalization continues, so does the demand for companies like freight brokerages, which enable businesses to continue operating globally while addressing problems such as entering new markets or expanding into international trade agreements. So, what's the takeaway here? Freight brokerages are here to stay. They have become an essential component of the global economy and will remain so for as long as there are international transportation needs.

Chapter 2: Why Become a Freight Broker

Many people working today are looking for complementary methods to increase their income. Freight brokerage is an excellent fit for people familiar with the trucking and transportation businesses because they will already have established contacts in their careers. However, even if you don't have much experience in the business, you can still learn to become a freight broker. This chapter will list the different reasons you should become a freight broker and outline a typical working day in a freight broker's life.

Benefits of Being a Freight Broker

In recent years, there has been a growing demand in the freight brokerage industry. The industry has been experiencing stability and growth with no significant fluctuations, which is why many people are considering changing careers to become freight brokers. Here are a few reasons why freight brokerage is the right move for you:

1. Freight brokerage does not require extensive special training or a particular degree. This means that any person can learn how to become a freight broker. This aspect is one of the main advantages of this industry because so many other careers require a university degree of at least four years. Even college graduates often still have to take a job at entry-level for several years before gaining enough experience to make a decent income.

You can do your own research and learn everything there is to know about freight brokerage as an industry. You can approach different professionals in the business and learn firsthand what it takes to become a freight broker. Instead of taking college courses and without any practical training, you can approach a few companies and ask to be an apprentice or an intern so that you can have hands-on experience.

Suppose you are already familiar with the business, for example having worked as a truck driver. In that case, the networking aspect is a lot easier because you will already have contacts to reach out to. The whole concept depends on whether you can deliver shipments and provide an open communication channel with your clients to establish a professional relationship built on trust.

2. Another major advantage of being a freight broker is that you don't need huge capital to get started. All you will need is a laptop, an internet connection, and a phone number. You don't need to pay a hefty sum for insurance, licenses, and other expenses that go into starting any business if you are already working with a professional freight broker.

You may work out a deal with them to represent their company while having your own clients. In return, they would get a commission fee or a percentage of your profits from each transaction. This is the perfect deal for you in the beginning, so you will not have to invest a large sum of money to get started. You can make enough money before you even separate your business from your current broker and build your own company with your existing clients.

Suppose your broker doesn't already have one for you. In that case, you could purchase a TMS (transportation management system) to facilitate communication between all parties in your business, from your shipping clients to your mobile carriers. Being an independent broker typically does not require a huge initial investment or monthly overhead to manage your business.

3. There is no limit to your income like when you used to work an eight-hour shift. You get paid each time you make a booking for shipping and see it delivered successfully to its destination. This is perfect for you as an independent agent as you can make as many bookings as you want, depending on the range of your contacts. You could start making anywhere from $60,000 to $150,000 in your first year, and the good news is that you can top it off as much as you like. A freight broker is an entrepreneur who is triggered by their motivational spirit. The whole business depends on your confidence to score bookings, and with a few pointers, you will be able to get the hang of it in no time and start making money.

4. You can work at any time of day without having to stick to a continuous eight-hour shift. You can divide the number of hours between day and night, or however many days of the week you work. However, you still need to put some effort in to get some decent revenue and maintain enough contacts to make bookings, but the idea is you'll have a flexible schedule to adjust to your liking.

You can take time off if you are overly stressed or sick and not worry about your annual leave with your boss. Your time off does not mean that you won't take bookings. You can hire a dispatcher during your time off to oversee the bookings process, and you can check in as minimally as you wish to make sure deliveries are made on time. Your transportation management system can help you manage your load board if you can't be available for a few days or a week.

5. You can work from the comfort of your own home in your pajamas. Nobody will be breathing down your neck because you didn't show up early at work. Amid the current pandemic conditions, a freight broker's career can continue without any delays because they typically work remotely. This will also save you the costs of commuting to and from work every day. This also means that you can work from anywhere, even if you decide to spend some time on a beach in Hawaii.

6. You don't have to work at a specific location or only take orders in your local business neighborhood. You can offer your services to anyone in the country, and as your company grows, you can expand to an international level. It is wiser and more manageable to start your business between cities or states as there is not a lot of complexity involved in the intrastate shipping process, but there are no limits to how far your business can reach. This makes freight brokerage a great fit for people who want to leave a mark on the market while operating the business from home.

7. The freight brokerage business is always in demand, which makes it an excellent opportunity to achieve growth in your business. The trick is to not settle for your current customers but to always look for new opportunities to expand your shipments and deliveries. Different opportunities will teach you which type of loads are the most profitable. This also means that you won't depend on a certain client and lose income if you can't make bookings with them anymore.

8. Being an independent freight broker allows you to live your life without wasting too much time commuting or working overtime at the office. It's a chance to be in charge of your own income and not have to answer to anyone. Working eight-hour or ten-hour shifts per day gives you a limited time to spend with your family or catch up on your favorite activities and de-stress from the long workdays. Being an independent freight broker helps you create a good balance between your career and personal life and allows you to alter your schedules to fit in important family events.

9. When you move on to being a business owner, you can create something for yourself and your family. You can hire employees within your family and make a name for yourself. You will know which member of your family can be a perfect fit for a position in your company. This becomes your legacy, which will be passed down to future generations.

What Does a Freight Broker Do on a Typical Day?

Freight brokers act as the middle person between shipping clients and carriers. They are responsible for arranging transportation to deliver shipments within a deadline. The idea may seem easy, but there are a few things to consider when establishing a successful business. As a freight broker, you'll have to keep up with the clients' requirements and the demands of the business. The best way to gain hands-on experience is to learn from an experienced freight broker. We will show you what a typical day looks like for a freight broker.

First, you'll be reaching out to customers who need shipments carried. Typically, you'll have a record of at least twenty shipping clients at the start. You'll need to have accurate information about the type of shipment, the type of vehicle required to carry the loads, and the pick-up and delivery locations.

A typical day for a freight broker may start as early as sunrise – but may start at any hour that works for calling clients and asking if they need transportation for their shipments. Your schedule is related to their schedule, around the time they start to place the finishing touches on their shipments. You may not score a booking with the first or even second client, but perseverance is key in this case. With enough customers in your database, you will almost certainly make a booking, if not several.

Once you make a booking, this is your time to shine. You need to ensure the shipment reaches its destination on time and ensure professional delivery with the cargo intact. When you've proven yourself to a couple of clients, they will start calling you to transfer their shipments and may even assign you several shipments per day.

When the shipper gets a load, you will take the order from them, and they will fill you in with all the necessary information. This is the time to exercise good communication skills as it is crucial to establish a good relationship with your clients. You will then have to give your dispatcher or trucker the exact information you received from the shipper and double-check that they do it right.

This is when you will work out your commission with the shipper. Your payment would be an estimate because it depends on the type of truck, amount of cargo, and the commute distance. In the beginning, you could ask the client what they are willing to pay. After a while, you will understand more about calculating your rate to achieve a decent profit margin after paying for the truck. A good starting point is to achieve a 10% margin per shipment.

It's important to record your progress on the load boards online. You can find numerous records for previous shipment deliveries on the load boards, usually accompanied by the trucks used to carry each shipment. This gives you a great database for truckers and carriers so that you can have numerous options to choose from, which will come in handy when orders start to pile up. The load board is also the perfect place for people to know you are in business, and they may respond to your posts and contact you for business.

Bear in mind that it might be tricky at first to find dispatchers or truck drivers to carry shipments. Some may be available but prefer not to drive long distances. It's important not to give up during these trying times because, with time and practice, you'll be able to expand your network of contacts and find more clients and dispatchers to keep the business running. It's important to have a large database of clients and truck drivers because they are the two main pillars of your freight brokerage business. The rest has to do with decent communication skills and being as organized as possible when it comes to taking care of different shipments simultaneously.

The idea is to take things slowly at first. It's important to work hard but not take on too many shipments. Don't be tempted to book too many clients if you still haven't gotten the hang of the business. Build your business slowly and steadily to ensure continuity. If you overwhelm yourself with orders, you may end up losing business because you may not be able to manage them all.

After finding a truck driver for the shipment, it's time to call the shipper to tell them you will take the shipment. You will send all the details to the carrier or driver by fax and ensure they have the proper approvals and insurance information before receiving the shipment and hitting the road. As the broker, you are responsible for ensuring the carrier has all the documentation they need for the shipment. You can contact the carrier online or by phone. After making sure the carrier has the proper documentation, you need to send them the final document to confirm the order. The carrier then signs the confirmation order under the current date and faxes it back to you.

When you receive confirmation for the order, you'll need to contact your carrier if they didn't already call you after confirming the order. This is the time to tell the carrier of the shipment details and whether there are any instructions involved. It's important to encourage the driver to call you if they face any trouble on the road. They should also contact you when the shipment is loaded on their truck and delivered to their destination. For trips across cities or states that take several days, your driver should call you every day to check in. This ensures an open communication channel with your carrier to achieve a smooth shipment delivery.

Once the driver notifies you that the shipment is delivered, you should get back to the shipper to inform them of the delivery. Suppose any problems occurred with the shipment, like part of the shipment being damaged or missing. In that case, the carrier is responsible for these problems. The matter should be resolved between the shipper and carrier, but sometimes you will be required to step in, for instance, if you neglected to inform the driver of the correct information regarding the cargo. This may include informing the carrier that the shipment is fragile or should be unpacked a certain way, the exact number of items in the shipment, or any other details that you failed to communicate to the carrier.

In this business, it's essential to stay alert at all times so that you can identify the source of a problem and fix it right away. Sometimes, deadlines won't be met or carriers won't show up to pick up the shipment. It's your responsibility to oversee anything related to the shipment from the time the carrier picks it up from the shipper until the time of delivery. With time and practice, you will be able to repeat the process and resolve any issues swiftly and efficiently.

A Success Story

The freight brokerage business sector is expanding, with over 17,000 brokers working in the United States alone. This means it is a booming but competitive industry, but there is still room for more brokers to establish a name in the market because demand for freight brokers is increasing. It's time to share a success story of one of the most successful companies in the business so you can have something to look forward to as a novice freight broker.

Scotlynn USA is a company that specializes in moving perishable products and is among the most successful companies in the country. However, they didn't start that way; they began their business as farmers who grew their own fresh fruits and vegetables and distributed them on their own. Their main produce was based in the winter season, so their trucks would be parked during the summer, which is why they thought of using their trucks in freight brokerage.

They already knew what the job entailed since they shipped their own products. This is why it was just common sense to open a trucking and brokerage company adjacent to their farming business. They had prior experience with customer service and already had their own network of connections, so scoring bookings was not difficult. They soon established a reputation for being the best produce transportation service and had to dedicate a whole department to transportation just to keep up with their clients' demands.

It's important to focus on what you know in this business. Not every broker starts with a well-established company, but that doesn't mean you shouldn't pursue your dream of becoming a freight broker. You need to start small and build your business from the ground up. It's not a good idea to take too many orders because you might struggle to handle the workload. Once you get the hang of taking one or two shipments per day, then it's time to reach out to more clients. When you have enough experience in the business, share your knowledge and expertise with your customers, which will help your marketing strategy as people will start spreading the word about your brokerage business.

This chapter discussed the most common advantages of being a freight broker and why it can be a great career move. We mentioned what a typical day looks like to give you an idea of what to expect in your day-to-day business. We encourage you to consider all the advantages listed in this chapter so that you can get a step closer to becoming your own boss by working as a freight broker.

Chapter 3: Building Your Empire

This chapter explains everything you need to know about setting up your business from scratch, from paperwork to registering the brokerage to choosing an agent for the company. You will also learn the key traits required to build a strong empire.

How to Start a Brokerage Business

A freight broker works as a middleman or intermediary between motor carriers and shippers. A motor carrier is a trucking company with trucks, whereas a shipper is someone with freight that needs to be moved. Therefore, a shipper hires a freight broker to connect them with a carrier. A broker's role is to facilitate the movement of goods. If you plan to operate a brokerage, there are different things you should do first, like obtaining licensing to hire contractors, independent agents, or employees.

Types of Brokerage Services

Freight brokers charge shippers more money than the truck's actual expenses, which is how they make money in their operation. If you want to open a freight brokerage company, the following are some of the business models you can consider:

Full Service

You can choose the freight broker business model of offering full service. With this model, the customers will get all the services they want from a single provider – you. For instance, you can offer consultancy services in addition to the standard logistics and perhaps target consumers in different regions. This model will give you a competitive advantage when you offer diversified services.

However, the challenge is that the customers' needs vary across regions. With a full-service model, you may end up holding something for which there is no demand. Therefore, you need time to understand the particular needs of clients from different places when you choose this business model.

Lane-Focused

This model identifies carriers that specialize in a specific area. For example, you can consider different freight categories like removals, heavy cargo, or consumables, and identify transporters who focus on each field. You can also make it easier to manage your logistics by looking for carriers that ply certain regions.

You should look for clients that share common interests. Since the freight market is volatile, you need to get as many customers as possible if you choose this business model. When you have a strong customer base, your business can enjoy stability.

Industry Focused

This approach to the freight broker business is based on specialized industry knowledge. With this strategy, you will build your customer base from a product or industry perspective. For instance, there are certain things you should know when dealing with industries that involve steel, apparel, construction, or produce. If you know about or learn about and then focus on one sector, you are likely to enjoy efficiency. This will give you a competitive advantage.

The trick is to find an industry you are interested in and already know about. It is imperative to learn different aspects of the business to gain a competitive edge. You must consider networking and reading the latest industry news to understand the business landscape.

How to Register Your Business

You should get all the paperwork required in your state or country to start up a freight broker business. This kind of business has a low barrier to entry, which means that many people can easily become freight brokers. The following are the major steps you should take to start your business:

Register the Broker Business

While starting a business is exciting, you need to decide the exact type of venture you want to focus on. You can register your business as a partnership, sole proprietor, or limited liability corporation (LLC). An LLC will limit your personal financial risk; sole proprietorships and partnerships are easy to set up, but they can expose you to financial liabilities likely to emerge from your business operations.

Apart from choosing the structure for your business, you also need to choose an appropriate name. You need to select something easy to identify in the market. Once you come up with a list of potential names, check to see if they are available, and don't use any names already registered. Try to find a unique brand name that can make you stand out from the rest.

Operating Authority

You must get authority to operate from the Federal Motor Carrier Safety Administration (FMCSA) or equivalent for your locale. You should pay an application fee and provide all the documentation, bearing in mind it can take between four and six weeks to have your permit processed. Before submitting your application, make sure you check the paperwork for any mistakes to avoid delays. You must keep a copy when you apply.

A Surety Bond

You must have a surety bond worth about $75,000 before you start operating your freight broker business. This money is meant to ensure that the trust fund or the bond company will reimburse the carrier if the freight broker fails to meet its obligations. You can get surety bonds via an insurance company or partnering with an insurance provider that offers freight broker bonds.

The law requires all freight brokers to obtain surety bonds, also known as freight broker bonds or BMC-84. You need to get complete details about different types of broker bonds to avoid penalties if you fail to meet the requirements.

Process Agents

Another crucial step you should take when building your business empire is to file a list of process agents with the responsible boards in your country. If you operate in different states, make sure you have process agents since they can provide court documents on your behalf in case of a lawsuit or any related court action. Process agents will also play a role in executing contracts on behalf of your company. Many clients will connect with your business via process agents located in different areas.

Ensure the process agents and other strategic employees receive adequate training to provide excellent service in your freight brokerage business. Check with your responsible authority to see if you have all the necessary licenses and permits required to operate your business. If you wish to grow your business and create an empire, ensure that all permits and licenses are renewed on time.

If you are a freight broker, you need to complete periodic updates and renewals of pertinent information like surety bonds. Do not wait for your registration to expire since this information must always be up-to-date. More importantly, your business must comply with the regulations and laws of the land.

How to Build Your Empire in the Freight Brokerage Business

When you have registered your business and obtained all the necessary licenses and paperwork to operate, you should aim to build an empire so that you become a force to be reckoned with in the industry. The following are some measures you should consider when building a successful trucking business:

Develop a Strong Business Plan

The first and most important thing to building an empire within the trucking sector is to create a ten-year business plan. This will help you determine the kind of trucks and equipment you will need to operate your business. When starting this type of business, make sure you have a manageable size of support staff to keep things running. It is always good to start small and gradually expand your operations as your business grows. You need to first see how the venture performs to make informed decisions.

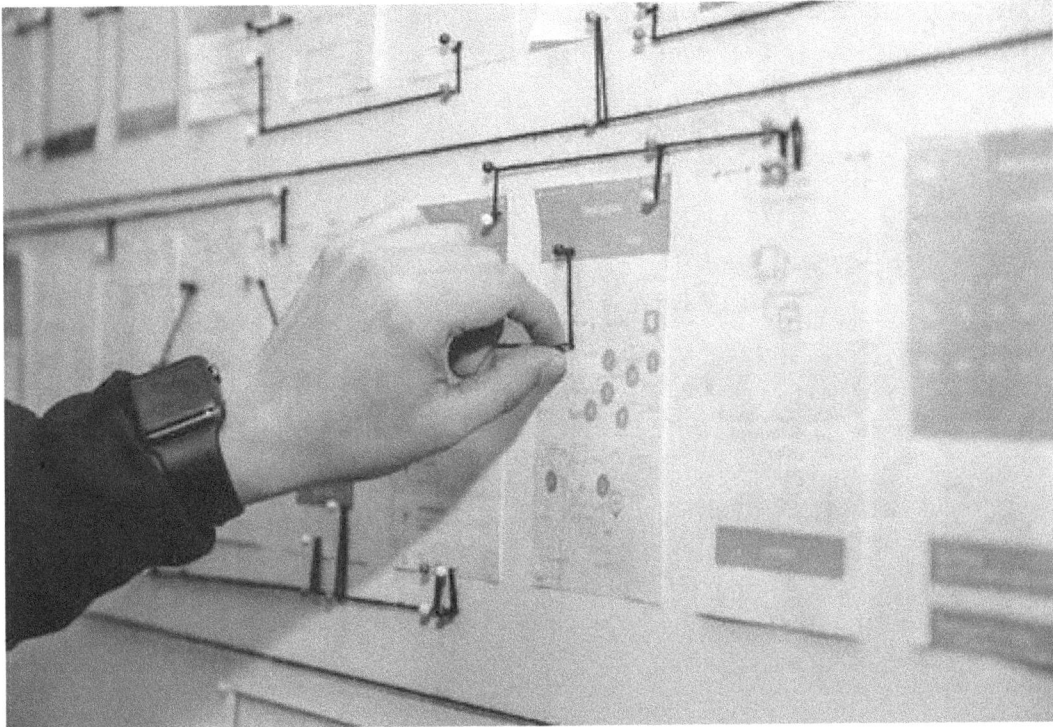

Hire the Right People

The success of your business depends on the quality of your workforce. While there are no special qualifications for a freight broker, make sure you recruit people with good industry knowledge. Check if the potential employees have prior experience in the logistics and freight sector. Try to select people who have worked as logistics managers, truckers, or someone with experience as a dispatcher.

Another element you can consider is offering ongoing training to the employees to understand how the industry functions. You can provide online training to benefit your agents based in different areas. Classes can only take a few weeks, focusing solely on procedural skills required to guide the transportation process smoothly.

With these courses, you can educate your employees about the types of transport required, regulations, contract types, invoices, and other essentials of running a freight brokerage. To achieve your goals, you should ensure that your workers receive constant training in different areas to help improve their overall operations.

Manage Your Trucking Fleet

When you obtain your permits and licenses, you need to determine the appropriate size and capacity of the trucking fleet to ensure that you build a formidable business. Depending on your budget, you need to decide if you wish to rent a fleet or purchase your vehicles. It becomes easier to run your brokerage if you have your own trucks instead of hiring vehicles.

The main advantage of owning trucks is that you can customize them to suit your business needs. For instance, if you are into the transportation of fresh produce, you can install refrigeration units in trailers or box trucks (ones you acquired at a better price than the same trailer/box truck with factory-installed units.) Your short-term goals and budget should help you determine the appropriate equipment you need in your operations. Effective fleet and inventory management are major components you should consider when running a successful freight business.

Build Contacts and Promote Networking

When you are a freight broker, you look for shippers who require transportation to move various goods. It is essential to build contacts in various regions to attract potential clients. You can use several methods, like networking, to generate leads for your business. You can use different social media platforms to connect with various people who can contribute to the success of your venture. Networking helps you build links with different people, and you can achieve this by attending workshops, business meetings, and other gatherings where you can interact with influential people.

The success of your business strongly depends on the marketing strategies you use. It would be best if you employed strategies like promotions and advertisements to create awareness among different people about the existence of your business and the services it offers. Email marketing is another method that can help develop your venture, especially when you show that you respect your clients. Happy customers will refer their friends and relatives to your business if they are pleased with your quality of service. You can also expand your customer list by emailing them and informing them about the services you offer.

SEO Strategy

In this digital era, you can utilize the search engine optimization strategy (SEO) to generate leads and, ultimately, conversions for your business. When customers are looking for services or products, they first look for information to help them solve their problems. SEO is designed to improve the ranking of your website in different search engine results. Blogs consisting of unique keywords play a role in improving your site's ranking and attracting many visitors.

If many people visit your site, some of them will try your offerings. These conversions are good for your business since they translate into more sales. Essentially, every business aims to generate revenue from sales. You can achieve this by providing valuable content to the target consumers, boosting your customer base. When the visitors to your site are happy about the information they get, they are likely to contact you, which marks the beginning of a lasting relationship. When you have loyal customers, you are likely to enjoy the steady growth of your venture.

Monitor Your Expenses

If you are concerned about making profits from your freight brokerage, you must exercise financial discipline. Learn to track all common expenses such as driver salaries, marketing, labor-related, fuel, and unforeseen expenses. It is imperative to sort the expenses of your business if you want to be in a better position to track your finances. Make sure to keep track of your cash flow and avoid the temptation of spending money on activities that do not add value to your operations. Make sure your business account is separate from your savings account to avoid wasting money on things that do not contribute to the growth of your empire. You must have sufficient savings to cushion your business if unexpected cash-flow challenges hit it. It is essential to balance the expected outflows and inflows within a given time frame.

All you need is to have a clear vision and choose efficient processes that can help you lower operational costs in whatever you do. It is good to automate repetitive tasks like sending promotional emails and other messages to keep in touch with your clients.

What Does a Successful Freight Brokerage Look Like?

When you have successfully established your freight brokerage, it should be characterized by quality customer service. Excellent customer support is the basic tenet of the trucking business since it is the customers that keep your company running. Suppose the consumers are happy about your service. In that case, they will continue doing business with your organization, and they are also likely to refer their peers and relatives. Loyal customers are good for the success of any company since they bring a steady flow of income. When your venture is customer-centric, you are assured of unlimited growth. To achieve this, you must focus on providing prompt service, offering great prices, and personalizing your services. It is essential to be proactive and organized to meet the customers' needs on time. Having a solid customer base and providing reliable service can help your business succeed. Some businesses fail solely because of poor service to their clients.

Customized Service

When you are in the freight business, you should know that you deal with different kinds of customers. Therefore, providing custom-made services can go a long way in building a good brand that will appeal to the interests of many people. This will also help you gain the customers' loyalty to uplift your business to greater heights. You should know your target consumers' needs and anticipate that they can change over time. You need to conduct regular market research to satisfy your clients' needs

Offer Affordable and Competitive Rates

When customers do business with your company, they look for competitive and affordable rates. Since the trucking industry is characterized by stiff competition, make sure you offer competitive rates to boost your business and attract many people. It is vital to do market research, understand how other industry players operate and design effective strategies to make you stand out from the rest. Make sure your rates are neither too low nor too high to generate fair revenue from your operations.

Technological Integration

The trucking industry is also adopting technological integration like any other business. If you want to succeed in your freight business, make sure your company is tech-savvy. You can make order processing and payments quick and efficient with the right technology. This will give your business a competitive advantage. You must also ensure that you respond to clients promptly and assist them with any needs they may have.

Employee Motivation

A successful business focuses on motivating employees and keeping them happy. Satisfied employees are productive, which helps your business generate more revenue and attract more customers. When you treat your employees like valuable assets, they will develop a sense of belonging to the organization. This will make them put optimum effort into their operations to help the firm achieve its desired goals. It is good to include the employees in the decision-making process to empower them in their operations.

Maintain a Constant Cash Flow

You must maintain a constant cash flow to ensure smooth operations. You must use the money to grow your business and ensure you do not get stuck when things are not going your way. When business is low, you need to find better ways to overcome the challenges without considering the option of borrowing.

Suppose you are interested in operating a successful freight broker business. In that case, it is vital to implement effective strategies that can help you build long-term relationships with clients. When you set up your business, you should target the right consumers. You can achieve this by using networking and other marketing strategies to target the ideal customers.

Chapter 4: Adapt or Perish

We can't deny the fact that the world is constantly changing. Even though the nature of the trucking business has remained relatively constant, the overall market within which freight forwarding services exist and the way they address consumer needs have changed drastically. In the last hundred years, the way businesses operate and the consumers they cater to have improved and have allowed the businesses to expand more than ever. Never before were economic circumstances as beneficial for commerce as there are today. At the same time, businesses are faced with all kinds of challenges that were also never present before.

A prime example of this is the recent pandemic of 2019, which no business could have predicted and whose repercussions were unlike anything we have experienced before. Even though there have been pandemics in the past, they were all quite a while ago, and the overall economic situation was quite different back then. Looking at recent economic data, it is easy to see that the past forty years have been the most profitable years for businesses across the world in the past couple of centuries. However, now we face a new set of challenges that could pop the high-profit bubble that businesses exist in today.

One of the most concerning factors today is growing competition. While we do have the largest consumer base at the moment, with more business and individual consumers around the world, at the same time, we also have the most competitive market in the world. This is the largest market there has ever been in terms of economic size and the number of competitors in the market. Moreover, it is no longer just the powerful western economies booming economic activity. Several upcoming economies are well on their path to overtaking the long-standing economic powers. For businesses, this means that the focus of economic activity is about to shift and might require them to drastically change the way they are structured within the markets to which they cater.

Also, it is important to note why the previous era of profitability occurred. Two of the main factors went hand-in-hand; the decrease in federal regulation and the privatization of businesses. This change of privatization and deregulation occurred just after the 1980s, when state-run entities were the norm. Private ownership of these large companies and less stringent legal frameworks allowed them to optimize their performance and turn into the profit-churning behemoths that they did. At the same time, this coincided with an incredible amount of urbanization and globalization. Businesses were transitioning to industrialization, there were more consumers to cater to, and the overall demand was now coming from the global market rather than just a limited local market.

Another factor that contributed to this change was the fact that the disposable income of the average consumer was rising quickly. While poverty was also increasing, we saw massive growth in the middle class, specifically in the class that made over $10 per day. Just forty years ago, about a billion people worldwide made over $10 per day, whereas today, that figure has risen to well over three billion. This increase in disposable income has a ripple effect across the global economy, and it is a change that positively impacts every sector.

Moreover, the kind of products we consume has changed significantly with developments in technology and business. Over the past four decades, we have seen an exponential rise in sectors such as oil, steel, cement, large capital projects, infrastructure development, power production, agriculture, consumer goods, and electronics and technology. An excellent example of this change in consumer behavior in recent times is the high rates of internet penetration in countries all over the globe, together with the high adaptability of smartphones and smart digital devices. A decade ago, internet and computer usage were a fraction of what they are today, and smart technology did not even exist.

One of the most significant changes in the recent few years for businesses and the economy's overall condition was the scale of operations. Modern tech giants such Apple and Google and large organizations from other industries such as Walmart and Exxon Mobil have turnovers that surpass the GDP of entire countries. Foxconn, a huge electronics manufacturer, employs more people than the total population of some countries. The scale of business is larger than it has ever been before, significantly influencing the unprecedented growth of modern organizations.

Changing Trends

The rising cost of operations is one of the most significant changes contributing to the drastically different economic environment we are experiencing today. Ever since World War II, as businesses were expanding to new regions and workers were coming from overseas to work in developed western economies, businesses had easy and plentiful access to cheap labor. Even relatively complex jobs that required skilled labor were done at a fraction of the price of local labor. This trend is slowly changing as we experience global inflation, a global market, and more physical mobility of labor. Moreover, the changes in worker availability are also driving workers to charge higher prices for their services. We can see this quite clearly in the trucking industry, where there has been a shortage of drivers for several years now, and the problem has worsened after the pandemic.

Secondly, economies that have peaked in performance usually have access to a young and productive workforce. Prime examples of this are China and nearly all western economies. Fifty years ago, when these countries had a working population mainly under the age of forty, they experienced very high levels of growth. Today this trend has changed, and the growth rate is falling quite sharply. In some regions, the growth rate has even become negative. Regardless, over the next fifty years, we will inevitably see a decrease in growth rates worldwide, and it will be very similar to what we were experiencing before the World Wars.

We can see that countries like China are now promoting having more children and trying to get younger people into the country to carry the burden of the economic machines that the previous generation helped build. However, this is proving to be much harder in reality. New workers have to face much higher costs than what they faced fifty years ago. They live a completely different lifestyle, and most don't see the value in working long hours for nominal wages. They are not motivated by the same factors, contributing to their unwillingness to work.

This presents a new set of challenges for businesses, and we can see that we are coming to the end of cheap labor and ever-decreasing production costs. Plus, there is another threat for businesses looming on the horizon.

Importance of Digitalization

The most significant change we are seeing right now is probably the internet. While this is a fantastic opportunity for smaller businesses to capture the global audience, it is also a threat for corporations because they will face more competition. Even though this competition might not be from large corporations, the fact is that when customers see more options, they are more likely to sway to a different seller. These smaller sellers also get more credibility when connecting to major online platforms such as Facebook, Alibaba, or Amazon.

Being present on these platforms eliminates the need to market their own website. It saves them the cost and time it takes to set up an e-commerce store, giving them instant access to millions and even billions of customers that are loyal to that platform. This can be more clearly seen in the value of digital businesses. In 1990, the e-commerce industry was worth less than $500 billion; in 2020, the same market was worth more than $5 trillion. Thanks to the internet, anyone can start a business from the comfort of their own home in a matter of minutes.

Why It's Critical to Market

Marketing has always been an essential part of any business operation. However, given the circumstances highlighted above, marketing is more important than ever, but how marketing is done will dictate the effectiveness of these efforts. For businesses to get the most traction they can, they need to stay in the public eye and show consumers why they are the best choice.

The internet has made digital marketing a little bit easier and a lot more cost-effective for businesses. Whether that is email marketing, digital ads, promoting your website, or advertising on different digital platforms, businesses can do this in various ways. The important thing to note is that while this is easy to get into and quite economical at the start, if a business really wants to harness the power of digital marketing, then they need to invest in this avenue.

Hiring the right marketing team is crucial for this operation. They will not only assist you in formulating a marketing campaign that will bring in more customers, but they will also assist you in understanding what your current marketing campaigns are lacking. They will use insights and feedback to highlight where your customers are and how you can target those customers more effectively.

Marketing Methods

It should come as no surprise that many of your potential customers are online. Today the internet is home to over four billion daily users, slightly over half of the total world population. Under the digital marketing umbrella, several categories can be used in conjunction with each other. You might want to focus on a specific solution and scale your operations within a marketing style.

One of the most common ways of marketing via a digital presence is through Search Engine Optimization (SEO). In a nutshell, this involves all the techniques that will help your web pages, your social media, and all kinds of other digital assets to show up in relevant search results. Nearly every internet user today relies on a search engine to find the information or resource they are looking for. There will be multiple sites that offer the information that the user needs for any search query. Using SEO, you can get your site to rank higher up in the search results and essentially have a better chance of being viewed.

Email marketing or email outreach is a way to develop a personal relationship with the customer. This is a step forward from SEO because now you aren't depending on the user to find you. Instead, you have direct contact with them through email. Just like how in the past, companies would email you the newsletter and all kinds of other material to keep you updated with what was going on, email marketing is a faster, cheaper, and more effective way of doing that. The main challenge is actually getting the customers' email in the first place. Different businesses have different ways of getting the users' email addresses, and this will depend mainly on what you offer and how your customers interact with you. However, once you have the email address, you can do a lot more than just send out weekly newsletters. There are many ways you can use email marketing. You can do everything from simply increasing brand awareness to developing a better relationship with clients to actively selling the products.

Social media marketing is another form of marketing that is picking up momentum these days. The main reason for this is that social media is becoming the norm. There are billions of people available on social media platforms, and if you can be present on all these platforms, you have access to all these clients. More importantly, it is a lot more streamlined than just being available on the internet. You exist in a closed ecosystem through social media where people can do anything, from learning a new skill to buying groceries to looking for people they knew from elementary school. Also, through social media marketing, you get a lot of information about your marketing campaign and the users to whom you are marketing. This is not so readily available when you are simply marketing through the internet. You can get similar results, but you will need several additional services, and you will need to know how to use them. Social media platforms give you all these resources for free, and you can use them to your advantage.

Content marketing involves using all kinds of content, whether written, visual, or audio, to let people know about your business and find new customers. You will be using some form of content marketing in any digital marketing you do. Just like how businesses use a mix of print media and TV to market in the physical world, you can use a mix of different content styles to engage the maximum number of people in the digital arena. You might be present on a video-sharing platform to showcase informative videos about your products. At the same time, you have a group of social media platforms where customers can come together and discuss your products and a team that creates informative written content. The latter is sent out through the mail marketing system to improve customer relationships and sell directly through their inbox.

Affiliate marketing is a line of work that has become quite popular with digital workers as they can sell the products of a different company and earn a commission on each sale. They are doing the same thing that sales reps would do in the physical world when they walk through neighborhoods knocking on doors and cold selling. The main advantage of doing it online is selling to a global audience. Rather than going through extensive digital marketing procedures to increase sales, they can start an affiliate program where other people take the job of selling the products, and businesses only have to pay them a commission on each sale. How the affiliate marketer sells the products and who they sell them to is not the concern of the product or service owner.

These are some broad categories of digital marketing that any business can use. There are also some more specific kinds of marketing, such as instant messenger marketing and mobile device marketing, that certain businesses use, but these might not be effective for everyone. Look into the different options, try them out, and see what works for your business.

Management of a Modern Organization

In some parts of the world, especially America, employees are trying to get out of the 9-5 routine. Especially after the pandemic, the resignation rates have gone through the roof, and an increasing number of people are looking for different ways to earn a living. Many people that have been in a particular profession for decades are also changing paths and looking for more convenient ways to make money.

This can be seen in the trucking business, where people simply aren't willing to work long hours as a driver anymore. The same is the case in the food and restaurant industry, where people don't want to be performing basic jobs and would much rather do something that doesn't require them to spend a certain number of hours at work each day.

Businesses need to find solutions that can evolve with the organization's structure to manage this change.

One of the core components of any business is accounting. It would be best to have people who can keep track of your cash flows, give you financial advice, and help make sure that the money is going where it should be going. However, there is no need to have an in-house team in this digital era. In fact, you don't even need to have your own accounting solution. This job role doesn't require the accountant to be on site. They can work remotely, as long as they have access to all of the information they need. You can hire someone to work remotely for your business, or you can buy an off-the-shelf solution that will take care of all your accounting needs. Many premade accounting solutions are very detailed and cover every aspect of finances you may need to attend to.

In the same way, the human resource department can be overhauled and changed. As more work is done remotely, you might not even need a full-fledged HR department to help you with staff management. You may even get away with one remote worker to manage employee problems.

One thing that has revolutionized business operations is data. If you are not already making use of data, then this is something that you need to look into and capitalize on. Through data, you can optimize nearly every aspect of the business and improve your spending. Whether that is customer data, business data, marketing data, or any other kind of information, knowing the numbers behind things gives you a clearer picture of what is going on. Today, many free and paid resources can help you compile this information that you can use to your advantage. While the world's largest companies have dedicated data-management staff and billions of dollars in budgeting for data processing, even small businesses can make use of this asset within their budget. Businesses need to realize the importance of forecasting. Being able to look into the future based on current trends, user behavior, and data, we can understand what we need to do to stay successful in the long run. The business environment is changing at a faster pace than ever, but at the same time, we also have more resources than ever to stay on top of these changes. It takes a proactive approach to ensure you have what you need to stay profitable tomorrow.

Chapter 5: Pricing and Competition

There isn't a single industry in the world where you won't face any competition. Whether you are selling hot dogs in the street or developing outer space solutions for interstellar travel, there will always be someone else doing the same or a similar business and possibly targeting the same clientele. The challenge here is not how amazing your product is or how well-built your organization is; it is how effective your pricing and competitive strategy are at attracting potential buyers' attention and, eventually, their business.

Pricing and competition are essential factors for any business. You will find multiple price points at which different products are sold in any product category. Take chocolate, for example. You can get cheap, often poor-quality chocolate, medium-priced, better-quality chocolate, and expensive higher-quality chocolate that few people can afford. The same rule applies to both consumable and non-consumable products of all kinds. The important thing to note is that there are multiple sellers in each price range, and wherever your product might be ranked in the price spectrum, you will have to tackle competition of a similar nature. Some companies expand their product vertically and compete with other products in higher and lower price ranges. Others focus on a specific price range and aim to expand their consumer base within that price bracket.

Together with competition, businesses also have to factor in that they are constantly facing changing operational costs, consumer behavior is constantly changing, the overall economic environment is changing, and laws and regulations pertaining to their industry are also changing.

Moreover, pricing and competitive strategies are dynamic elements of the business. Depending on market conditions and the requirements of the business, these things can change, and they often do. Being flexible is vital for businesses to stay relevant in their spaces. However, some companies prefer to maintain a consistent pricing system and seldom change their competitive strategy. It's all about what works for you and how you can optimize certain aspects of pricing and competition to yield the most value for your business.

Let's look at how you can use pricing and competitive strategies to your advantage.

Competition Strategies

Competitive strategies are forms of management, operational processes, initiatives, business approaches, and tangible and intangible changes made to a business to achieve better business growth, improve market share, win over customers and clients, and surpass other competitors' businesses. In this regard, the management of a company and the people behind different operations in the business are of significant importance when it comes to implementing a solid competitive strategy. There may be situations in which the competitive strategy requires more input from one team than the other and other situations in which the entire organization is equally balanced.

Whatever the situation is, the aim is also for this strategy to be a sustainable activity and one that actively helps build a competitive edge. A business can employ various tactics to measure the success of such a strategy. For instance, a growing number of customers might be seen as growth, but this might not be a good sign if the per-customer revenue falls. It might be more critical for some businesses to improve customer retention, such as membership-based businesses where clients buy subscriptions. Businesses often aim to have customers that continue to use their services over a long period rather than having new sign-ups with high fall-out rates. Depending on the situation and the requirements of the business, there are a few different strategies that businesses can choose to adopt.

Cost-Leadership Strategies

Cost leadership strategies are all about maximizing economies of scale to produce products and services at the lowest price possible. Regardless of the price bracket within which a company is selling its offering, it will aim to be the cheapest option within that price range or try to offer more value than competitors at the same price. This is a widely used solution in markets with no price elasticity for the end product and in situations where the only way to compete is through mass volume. For instance, in the fuel industry, petrol stations try to charge as low as possible while marketing their product to be superior to others in the kind of performance benefits that it offers and how it will improve the engine's reliability. Generally, the price of fuel across different states and even in different parts of the same city will vary but only by a small amount. This is not enough of a difference for anyone to really profit from. As regulations on fuel prices are set by the government, the only real solution is to purchase cheaper raw materials and decrease fuel processing costs.

Businesses that adopt this model usually try to improve their purchasing, manufacturing, delivery, and local operational cost. These are often the most expensive parts of the production process, and using more machinery can drastically reduce costs in the long run. However, the problem with this approach is that it is relatively easy to copy. It is only a matter of time before a competitor achieves the same economies of scale or produces the product at a lower price. Customers who enjoy products made with this strategy in mind are usually looking for a specific product that isn't sold with any bells and whistles and is all about penetration pricing.

This is extremely effective in warding off new entrants to the market as businesses that have a smaller investment, or those whose operations are not quite at the same scale will find it challenging to compete with these super-sized firms. In a way, this opens the door for monopolies and creates the kind of environment that makes it easier for existing large firms to simply buy out the less profitable competition and integrate those operations to reduce their own costs further.

A significant challenge in this operation is the risk of the investments. Typically, solutions that will allow a business to reduce its operational cost will involve large capital investments. If things don't pan out or the business takes a different direction, this investment will be wasted.

Focus Strategies

Focus strategies are all about narrowing down your efforts towards a specific segment of the market, sector in the industry, price point, type of product, or any other specific area that you can focus on. For instance, a company may develop a focus strategy on a specific price point. If there are competitors' similar products within a certain price bracket, they might want to dominate that specific bracket. They will focus on expanding their reach at that price so that their product or service is the most bought.

In other cases, a business may want to focus on selling its product to a certain demographic. For instance, a company can focus on selling within a particular city and being the most-bought product of that category in that specific city. Similarly, businesses can focus on a certain kind of product, focusing on any niche and aiming to dominate that sector. This also helps to narrow down the research required for that business. Suppose a business only aims to dominate the market within a particular city. In that case, they need to only concentrate on studying competitors within that city and study how business is happening within that geographic area. In the same way, they can focus on specific aspects of the industry and aim to study those things exclusively to formulate their own strategy about how they will overcome those challenges.

Differentiation Strategy

This is when a business uses one of its services in a more excellent camouflage to target customers looking for higher-value products. For instance, Land Rover started life as an off-road vehicle manufacturer; however, this was not the most profitable segment, so they expanded their horizons to create more luxurious off-road vehicles. Over time, they have built a reputation for creating one of the most luxurious off-road machines, the Range Rover. In this way, they target a select range of customers that have the capital to afford a luxurious vehicle. Many other companies and even individual service providers will opt to cover similar unique offerings that will make them stand out in the market, and people will be willing to pay a premium for it.

Another example is how Lenovo has patented its classic keyboard design. While it is only a slight change from the standard keyboard, this has become a strong, unique selling point for their business, and many professionals swear by this kind of keyboard. In an industry such as laptops and computers where the hardware is often generic, having a unique selling point like a patented keyboard can powerfully attract clients.

Pricing Strategies

Many businesses don't pay sufficient attention to their product prices, even though those prices reveal a lot about their business to the buyer. Whether it is products or services, the way you price your goods can either earn you the right amount of money, push customers away, or leave you with less-than-optimal levels of profit. Moreover, the price that you charge also reflects the value your products or services will give to the customer. This definitely needs to be well-thought-out, and you should not be afraid to change it over time to get the most that you can from the market.

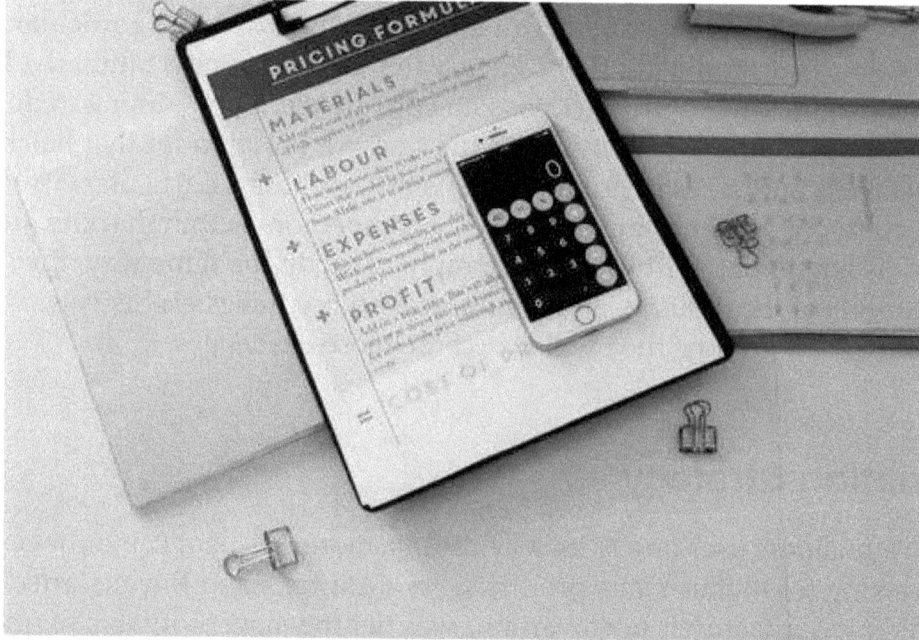

Pricing strategies can be tailored to suit specific business needs or modified to meet changing market conditions. Here are a few of the most common and most effective pricing strategies businesses use:

Penetration Strategy

It can be very challenging for businesses to enter the market in tight industries such as the tech space or the natural fuel industry. This problem is made worse because products are often very similar, and it is challenging and often expensive to create a unique offering through the product or service alone. In such circumstances or situations where the business just wants an easy entry into the market, they will price their products significantly lower than the competition. This has two benefits. Firstly, it is a great way to attract consumer attention. Customers are instantly drawn to something significantly cheaper in a market full of products within a specific price range. Secondly, since the price is much lower, it is a great incentive to try it out. They would be more risk-averse and choose a product they are already familiar with if the price was close to that of products they already use.

Sometimes businesses, just to get customers to try the product, will offer a smaller version of their product that is lower priced and hence an easier purchase decision for customers. The challenge in this situation is that businesses will barely be making a profit and might even risk the chance of incurring losses if sales don't meet a specific volume. Secondly, it can be challenging to retain customers when prices go up. Suppose the customers don't continue to buy the product when the pricing is moved higher. In that case, it can be difficult for the business to survive in the long run. Developing customer loyalty while raising prices is also challenging. Lastly, the low initial price can put some people off, and they might not purchase the product, thinking it will be a low-quality purchase. Moreover, the consumers might start to perceive the product as a low-value product, and when the prices eventually do rise, they will think that it is simply overpriced and isn't worth the additional cost.

Skimming Strategy

In a way, price skimming is the opposite of penetration pricing. Rather than starting at the lowest price possible, businesses start at the highest price possible, sometimes charging even more than the most expensive products in the category. This limits the buy to only those customers with the most spending ability, yet it also allows the business to "skim" the highest profit margin possible. In some cases where the production costs are high, the business might not be making the highest possible profit, but they will still be able to interact with those buyers that don't mind spending more money. Over time, the business will lower its price so that the product or service becomes available to lower levels of buyers with a smaller propensity to spend. In this way, the business can skim the full spectrum of buyers, and it's possible to circulate the product into every customer category. However, this is a rather risky way of pricing products and does not necessarily favor every kind of product. When done correctly and used for the right industry, it can be a fantastic way to scale the business and generate a lot of revenue.

Dynamic Pricing

In this form of pricing, the business is constantly changing the price that they demand for their offering. In cases when demand is low or there is an excess of supply, the price drops; when demand is high or supply is short, the price starts to increase. Again, this can be very effective when applied to the right industry. For instance, this is used very profitably for fuel, fresh vegetables, and fresh flowers. There are countless sellers for products such as fuel; they all have access to the same supply source at nearly the same costs, so it makes sense for them to fluctuate pricing according to the current market demand. On the other hand, fresh products that don't have much shelf life need to be sold as fast as possible, so dynamic pricing is critical. Dynamic pricing for products such as gym memberships is far from optimum, as people generally expect that the membership price will stay the same for the entire year.

SWOT Analysis

SWOT analysis is a framework that companies use to identify their Strengths, Weaknesses, Opportunities, and Threats (SWOT). This framework is a great way to analyze how the business is performing internally and how it measures up against the competition. It also helps the business know what to do to improve its performance in its respective market. This form of analysis can be made even better by using solid statistics and research-backed information that can be found about your industry, your type of business, and even the kinds of products and services that you sell.

It's also a great way to forecast things in your business and create a roadmap of what you might expect to happen in the future. Using this information, you can devise strategies that will help you counter possible problems and challenges and create solutions within your business that can help cushion against these changes. Today, we live in an era where we have easy access to all kinds of information from all parts of the world. Whether you want to expand or you just want to have a more in-depth ten-year plan, you can do everything that you need to prepare for that change through SWOT analysis.

Chapter 6: All about Business Plans

A business plan is a document that outlines the goals and objectives of your company. It also includes financial projections, marketing plans, and other information needed to help you achieve success. To start a successful freight brokerage business, you must first create a solid business plan.

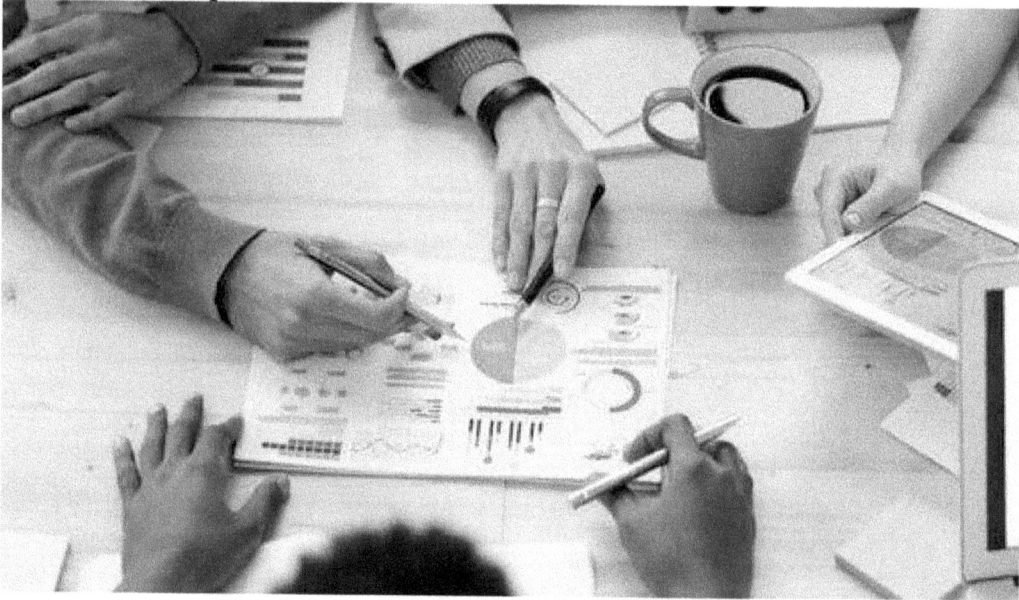

This chapter will discuss what a business plan entails. We'll talk about why they are important, how to get started on one if you want your new freight brokerage company to succeed, examples of what should go into them, and tips from experts on making sure yours has all the necessary components. At the end of this chapter, we will provide an example template that readers can use to start their own freight brokerage business plan.

What Is a Business Plan?

A business plan is a written document of your goals and ideas for the future. It should include an overview, strategies to meet each goal, financial estimates, and information about you or your company, including management abilities, strengths, and weaknesses. A good basic business plan also includes action plans that are necessary steps needed to be taken to reach your goals.

It should include a SWOT analysis, which is the process of looking at things from both an internal and external perspective to understand the various strengths, weaknesses, opportunities, and threats in your business world. A SWOT analysis can help you identify where improvements need to be made or where opportunities lie.

The SWOT analysis can help you determine the following:

- Strengths of your company and what makes it competitive in its industry.
- Weaknesses that need to be avoided, improved upon, or turned into strengths using other resources available to you through your network.
- Available opportunities because of changes or trends occurring in your marketplace right now (e.g., technology, legislation) and those that may occur later due to changing conditions such as demographics.
- Threats from both inside and outside forces, including new competitors entering the marketplace, technology advances by existing competitors, etc.

Why Is It Important to Have a Business Plan?

Having a business plan is essential because it allows you to focus on what your company will look like in the future. It also gives potential investors an idea of where they can expect their investments, time, and money to take your freight brokerage service, making them more likely to invest with you.

Additionally, having a business plan provides for strategic planning. Each decision made by your company considers how it fits within the framework of your overall vision and the steps needed to achieve said vision over several years. Managing daily decisions based solely on current conditions could spell disaster without a long-term strategy, so make sure to consider all aspects of your business when you're making plans.

The process of writing your business plan will also help you to fine-tune all the details involved in starting a freight brokerage service by helping you figure out what is essential and where additional resources are necessary. Once everything has been written down, it makes it easier for everyone involved to work together towards common goals.

How to Start Making a Business Plan

Ask yourself the following questions:

- What is my goal for starting a freight brokerage business? Why do I want to start this type of company in particular? How does it fit into the current marketplace, and what will set me apart from current competitors?
- Who exactly am I targeting as potential customers or investors, and why will they be interested in investing in/using a new service/product such as mine over existing ones that have been around longer?
- Which resources do we currently have available at our disposal, including personnel, equipment, technology, etc.? Do we need any additional help from

outside sources such as consultants or other companies who may specialize in areas where we have little or no expertise?

- Is my team ready to make the necessary sacrifices and commitments towards this type of business? What do we need to be fully prepared for getting started?

- What resources will be required to get started, and how quickly do we need them?

- Which steps are necessary for us to reach our goals after getting things off the ground, and what specific milestones must be met along the way?

- How long am I expecting this business to take before it becomes profitable or generates enough income/revenues that would make continuing operations worthwhile (for example, breaking even)?

Now, once you have the answers to these questions, it's time for your team to get started on creating a business plan!

The first step in laying a solid foundation on which to build should be determining what type of freight brokerage service you will provide. Will you be a carrier, broker, or independent service provider? This decision will affect many aspects of your business, including which type of insurance is necessary and who your customers/partners might be.

Once this has been figured out, it's time to map out the details such as:

- The different types of freight services that you will offer.
- The different types of customers you'll work with, including direct shippers or brokers who service indirect ones, and how each category will be serviced in a way that makes sense for both sides. How much does it cost? How long does the process take from start to finish? What about customer support throughout the process?
- The different types of contracts you'll use, including the length of contractual obligation, services included, and how much extra they will cost if any extras are needed. What kind of service level agreements (SLAs) can your customers expect to receive in addition to what has already been promised? How does this affect pricing structures, etc.?
- How you'll handle the different payment systems, including in-house credit card processing and/or third-party providers, and how it will all be integrated with your existing system.

Sub-Sections in a Business Plan

Now that the foundation has been laid out, it's time to start working on sub-sections of your plan, which will cover everything from sales and marketing strategies to how you expect growth to be handled over time.

Executive Summary

The first sub-section should include an executive summary that provides a brief overview of your business plan, including the type of freight brokerage service you'll offer and how many customers and partners it is expected to draw in over time.

Things to include in the Executive Summary:

- How do you plan to stand out from your competitors regarding services offered, pricing structure, and customer support? Why should customers choose you over others?

- What kind of growth do you expect to see over time through organic means (word of mouth) or advertising campaigns that bring in new business?

- The different types of customers you'll be working with; who are the big players? What is their common denominator in terms of logistics needs, etc.?

- The different channels through which your services will be marketed (online marketing? Social media campaigns? Local networking events?).

- Mission statement/overarching goals for the business.

- Business name, location, website address.

- The types of equipment that will be required to get started, including vehicles and office space (if applicable). What is the timeline for purchasing this equipment?

Description of the Company

This section is all about the different types of freight brokerage services you'll offer. It's important to lay this out in detail, including speed, accuracy, and any additional value-adds (such as customer support).

Things to include:

- How many employees/contractors do you plan to work for your company?
- How long have the founders of this business been involved in freight brokerage services? What are their backgrounds, including education, experience, and any certifications or accreditations they hold?
- Structure of the company, including ownership, legal status, and business structure.
- Details about your services, including the different types of freight you will be moving, speed, and accuracy when it comes to quoting. How do you ensure that all quotes are accurate? What kind of customer support is available if there are any issues along the way?
- The different types of customers you'll be working with. Who are the big players? What is their common denominator in terms of logistics needs, etc.?

Details about Services and Products

This section is all about the services and products you'll offer as a brokerage firm. It's important to lay out what kind of service your business will provide, including who it's targeted towards (audience) and any additional value-adds such as enhanced customer support or faster delivery times.

Things to include:

- What is the service you'll offer (in detail)? What are some of your key features/value propositions that set you apart from competitors?

- Unique features of the service, including speed, accuracy, and any value-adds.

- Does it come with any additional value-added services such as enhanced customer support, faster delivery times, etc.? How do these work, and what kind of impact will they have on customers?

- Lifecycle of this service, including distribution channels and customers.

- The pricing structure of the services and delivery times, etc. Does it come with any additional costs? Who are your key partners/vendors that you work with to ensure timely deliveries?

- Copyrights, patents, trademarks.

- You must address any legal concerns in terms of licensing or permits required to operate this business. Will there be any additional fees associated with these?

Overview and Detailed Analysis of Your Market

This section is all about the market that you will be targeting. What are some of the most important factors to consider when getting started with a freight brokerage firm?

Things to include:

- What kind of demand exists for your services in this market? Who are your key competitors, and how do they compare in terms of pricing and services offered?

- What kind of trends exist in this market, and how do they affect your business? Are there any new opportunities that might present themselves given these trends (e.g., the rise of e-commerce)?

- Marketing strategy, including online marketing and social media campaigns.
- Partnerships with other businesses in the market (if any). Who are they? What is your role as a brokerage firm among these partners?
- Macroeconomic factors that may impact this business, such as recessions, interest rates, etc.? How might these affect your operations or strategy moving forward?
- Risk factors present in this market, including legal issues, competition, etc. What kind of risks exist, and how will you mitigate these moving forward? What are some potential outcomes if these risks materialize?
- Future outlook and predictions for this market and your business.
- Detailed competitor analysis, including their strengths and weaknesses.

Competition Analysis

This section is all about competitor analysis, including their strengths and weaknesses. It's essential to have a detailed understanding of the competitive landscape before starting this business or marketing it, so including competitor analysis in your plan is crucial for success moving forward.

Things to include:

- Who are some key competitors? How do their strategies compare to yours? What are each competitor's strengths and weaknesses relative to your own business?

- Detailed analysis of each competitor, including how they market, who their target audience is/how you can differentiate, etc. What are some of the key reasons for differentiation between companies in this space? How do these strengths help them succeed moving forward? What kind of impact does this have on their overall business?

- How do you plan on competing with these firms, and how will that impact your strategy moving forward? What kind of differentiation between the two companies can be created to help establish a competitive advantage for yours? What areas of focus should we prioritize as we begin developing our market position within this space?

Business Strategy

This section is all about your business strategy. It's important to have a clearly defined set of goals and objectives that you are looking to achieve by getting started with this freight brokerage firm – an operating plan for the first year or so.

Things to include:

- Your short-term and long-term goals for this business, including financial projections if possible. What are some of the key strategies you'll be focusing on to achieve these objectives?

- What are some of the key assumptions that you must make to determine whether or not your business is viable?

- How do you plan on growing this business over the next few years, including hiring, expansion, etc.? What resources will be required for these goals, and how will you finance them moving forward?

- Any operational details related to this plan, including staffing, office location, etc.

- Detailed marketing and sales strategy for the business over the first year or so of operations. Who are your key partners? What kinds of partnerships with other businesses in this space might help you gain traction more quickly? How do these work, and what kind of impact will they have on your business?

- Social media strategy, online marketing plan, etc.

Financial Projections

This section is all about the financial projections for your business. It's important to include detailed cost, revenue, and profit figures that will allow you to determine whether or not this business idea would be profitable in practice.

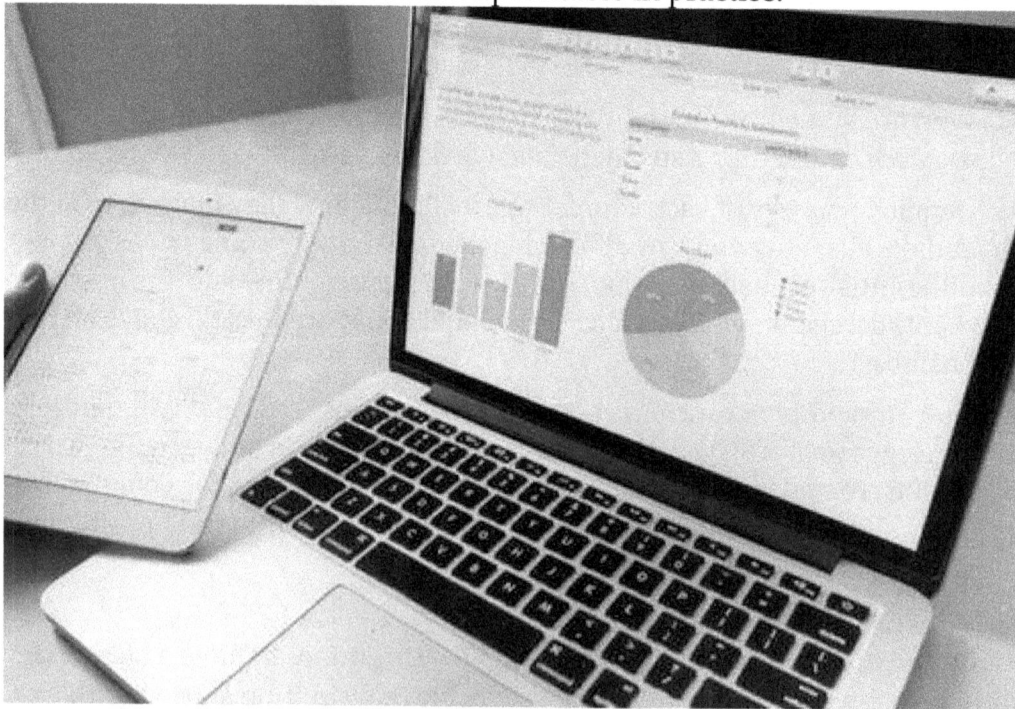

Things to include:

- Detailed sales, marketing, and operational costs associated with starting up and running the firm. What are some of the key assumptions you must make to determine if this business is viable moving forward?

- Break-even analysis. When does your firm start becoming profitable? What factors contribute to reaching break-even, and what impact do they have on these costs/revenue figures?

- How will you finance this business, including loans, investors, etc.?

- Any other financial details related to the projections. How will you make money? What kind of revenue/profit margins do you expect? How quickly will your sales volume grow over time relative to the costs associated with starting up and running the business?

How to Make Your Business Plan Stand Out

Every business has its own unique story to tell. And if you're writing your marketing plan or business plan, you need to choose the right words that will best describe who you are and what makes your company different from others.

Here are a few tips to help you out in presenting your company in the best possible way:

- Think about what makes your business special and unique. What are its strengths? How does it stand apart from other businesses in the same industry or niche?

- Don't just explain how your freight brokerage firm operates but also show potential clients why they should hire you instead of your competitors.

- Use the right tone and language that best reflects your customers' expectations, what they want to hear from a company like yours, and how you can help them achieve their goals.

- Ask an expert to vet your plan to make sure it is well-written, easy to understand, and visually appealing.

- Portray your business in a way that will make your potential customers more interested in learning about who you are and what you do.

- Write your plan with passion, authenticity, enthusiasm, and commitment to easily capture the attention of existing clients and new prospects.

How to Present a Business Plan to Stakeholders

Your stakeholders must understand how the company plans to achieve its goals and objectives.

So, when it comes time for them to review a business plan, make sure that they have an easy-to-read document, which includes plenty of visuals such as graphs, charts, etc., to quickly get all the information they need in an easy-to-understand format.

Also, your plan must be actionable, so all the stakeholders can develop a joint strategy to help you achieve each of these goals and objectives on time.

When stakeholders read your plan, they should feel like they are a part of the process and understand exactly what is expected of them.

Explain how each action contributes to a successful outcome by showing the benefits of implementing each change and demonstrating how it will lead towards achieving specific milestones outlined in your business plan.

Make a short presentation of your plan, so the stakeholders can ask questions and better understand what you're trying to achieve.

Show an accurate picture of your business and communicate it with passion, authenticity, enthusiasm, and commitment.

Be ready with a plan B in case something goes wrong along the way.

One-Page Business Plans

If you find writing a more extensive business plan too time-consuming and overwhelming, then try creating one that is just one page long.

This makes it easier for stakeholders to get the gist of your company's operations without spending hours trying to understand what your business does or how it operates.

Just like with any other type of business plan, your one-page business plan should include all the necessary details that will help stakeholders understand what makes your company unique and how it plans to achieve its goals.

You need to provide readers with enough information about who you are as a freight broker company so they know why they should work with you instead of other businesses in the same industry.

After the presentation, your stakeholders should provide you with valuable feedback and suggestions on how they can help take your business to the next level.

The most important thing is to have a plan. Without one, there's no clear way of knowing if you are on the right track or not. A business plan can help you make decisions by forecasting your future and laying out what needs to be done for it to happen. It's best to create one before you even begin your business. Not only does it help in the planning process, but it also allows for a lot of flexibility and change as you go along.

Printable Business Plan Template

Name of the Company	
Business Overview, Vision, and Mission	
Team Members	Experience and Roles in the Business
Description of the Company	
Service/Product Description	
Market Analysis	
Competitor Analysis	
Business Strategy	
Goals	
Success Metrics	
Probable Timelines for Achieving Goals	
Financial Projections	

Revenue Lines	
Cost Structure	
Profitability Plan	

Chapter 7: The Cost of Starting Up

Getting into the trucking business is no doubt going to be one of the most profitable decisions you will ever make, but it doesn't come without a rather heavy investment of both time and money. While it may seem like a relatively straightforward thing to do, a vehicle and a commercial driver's license are NOT all you need. If you plan to pursue this as a full-time business rather than just a side hustle, it will take a bit more work. Given that you may be transporting hazardous and valuable materials and may require special permits to operate the freight business, it will be beneficial to know the best way to go about these things. More importantly, as a person who will be spending more than fifteen hours a day at this job, it will also help to know how you will cope with this extremely taxing lifestyle and how to make the transition as smooth as possible. In this chapter, we will get into a bit more detail about what you need to get your business off to a great start.

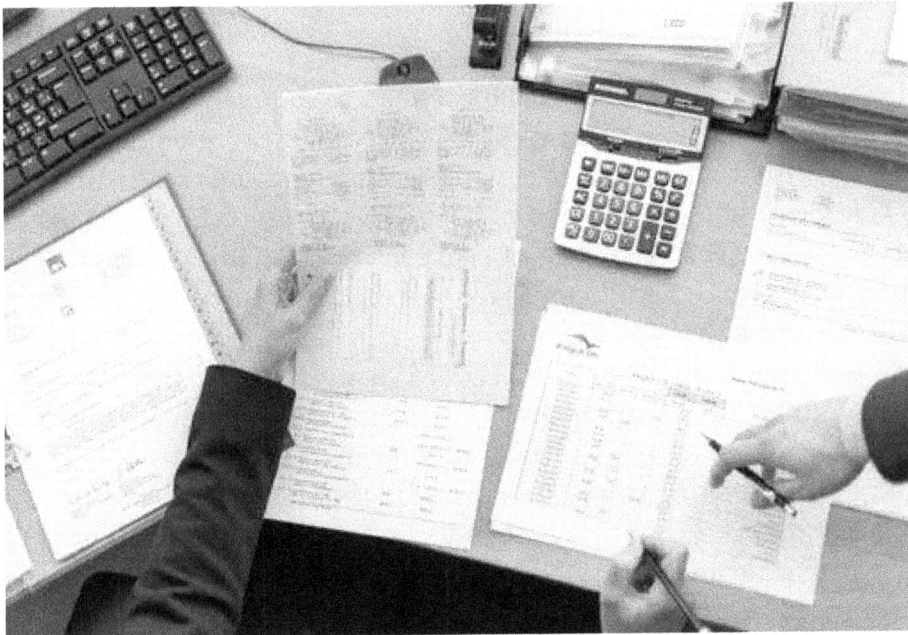

Things That Need to Be Done

Business Plan

Having a solid business plan will be especially important if you need to apply for any kind of financing. Whether this is financing for the business premises, the vehicles, or operational capital in any capacity, you will have a hard time convincing potential lenders without a well-thought-out and realistic business plan. Ideally, it would be best to work with a professional who has some experience in this industry or a specialist in the transport industry. Hiring a professional will be more expensive than going for a free business plan template online, but it will be well worth your money.

More importantly, this will be the first big milestone that will help you plan for the future and clarify what exactly your goals are. This doesn't have to be the final business plan, but you need at least a rough draft to get things off the ground. Suppose you are going to be using this plan specifically for financial purposes. In that case, you should forecast a minimum of three years, though forecasting for five years is optimum. This phase will take some research, so be sure to take your time. The time you invest in researching your business plan will also help you get familiarized with the best sources of information that you can use further down your business journey.

Paperwork

With your business plan in place, you will first need to start creating the legal infrastructure for your trucking business to get the company registered and set up as an LLC, Limited Liability Company. Even if you are starting just as an owner-operator, having an LLC in place will create a boundary between yourself, your personal assets, and the company assets. This is important because your personal assets will be protected if anything goes wrong with your business. As a trucking company, everything from your vehicle to the assets that you are moving is quite a high-value investment.

If anything were to go wrong with them, it could easily cost your car, your personal wealth, or even your house. To set up an LLC, you have to contact a registered agent. This is the requirement in most states, though you can look it up for your area and see what you need to do. More importantly, make sure that your registered agent is local and readily available at the company's physical address. Through this profession, you will be able to interact with state and federal laws. This means the agent must be there to receive and sign the following documentation:

- Legal notices
- State regulations and mandates
- Tax documents
- Paperwork related to your payroll or wage management
- Any other kind of business-related paperwork that needs to be processed by the agent.

If you fail to do so, the authorities will see it as a legal lapse, and you could be facing serious legal consequences. In some cases, failure to accept notices by the agent could even result in a lawsuit initiated without your knowledge. A seasoned agent will be aware of all these intricacies, and with the right professional, there will be nothing to worry about.

Next, you also need to apply for and collect an Employer Identification Number (EIN). This number reflects your businesses identity, much like how social security numbers are used for humans. This information is critical when you want to open a bank account, when you need to file taxes, and when you do anything that requires your business information. This simple nine-digit number is issued once, which stays the same as long as the business exists.

Licenses and Permits

As a transport company, there are quite a few different licenses and permits that you will need to get before you commence operations. Also, make sure you get in touch with the business registration team and find out what they need during your business registration process. Some permits will be preliminary requirements for the actual business registration, so you might need to apply for these before applying for business registration.

The most basic kind of legal document that you need is a commercial driver's license and the right endorsements. The state usually issues endorsements; depending on the kind of material you are moving, you might need to apply for specific approvals. Some endorsements you can just apply for and receive them. Others might require you to physically demonstrate your abilities, much like a driver's test, while others might require you to demonstrate your driving skill *and have a written examination*. So, read up on the endorsements you are looking for and apply for them accordingly.

Another number you need is the USDOT number allotted by the Federal Motor Carrier Safety Administration (FMCSA). This unique number will identify your trucking business and is used by the authorities when conducting any kind of inspection, audit, or evaluation.

Also, you will need an MC number, which is also known as the Motor Carrier Operating Authority number. Depending on your state regulations and the nature of your business, you might need to have more than one MC number.

When you get a process agent, you will also need to give them the autonomy to create a BOC-3 form (also known as a "blanket of coverage") on your behalf. This form is filed with the Federal Motor Carrier Safety Association (FMCSA), and your process agent will have to do it. Also, you are only allowed to file one copy of the form with the FMCSA, and it should outline all the states within which you operate. A separate copy of that form should be maintained at the main office of the freight-forwarding business or the broker. You should get an agent who can process this form for all the states you need to operate in.

Lastly, you will need some International Registration Plan (IRP) credentials and an International Fuel Tax Agreement (IFTA) form. If you are only operating within a single state, you might not need this, but this will be necessary if you operate in multiple states. Also, if you plan to travel through different states, you will need interstate permits.

Training

According to the most recent rules published by the FMCSA, drivers do not need to undertake any kind of training before applying for their commercial licenses unless otherwise stated in the state requirements. If a person wishes to get a CDL, then the first thing to do is to obtain the local CDL manual for that state and look into what kind of driver's license will be most appropriate for them.

Next, they must pass the state written test and then apply for the commercial learner's permit. Finally, they should have the permit at least fourteen days before the actual skills test, and the final step of the process is to pass the skills test.

It's also important to note that a driver's previous driving history will be evaluated when applying for the CDL. Even when trucking companies start hiring drivers, they will be subject to various FMCSA rules before hiring a person to drive their vehicles. If you are an owner-operator, it will be beneficial to look into this to ensure that your LLC is on the right path, and it will also give you some guidelines about what you should be aware of if you want to hire staff for your business.

If you already have an existing CDL or want to renew an outdated CDL, you will be subject to these new requirements. Moreover, if you are looking to get additional endorsements, such as those required to transport hazardous materials, you might be subject to the new regulations. However, before applying for any other application, make sure you look into your federal laws to see what applies to you.

If you are looking to apply for a Class A CDL, you must have at least thirty hours of driving time from a training school that is certified and accredited by the FMCSA. This includes at least ten hours of driving the truck in a practice driving range. This covers the requirements for driving a truck and trailer with a total weight of 26,001 pounds or more. If you are looking to apply for a Class B CDL, the requirements are somewhat more relaxed. You still need driving hours from a certified school, but only fifteen hours; out of these, seven hours should be in a practice range. This is the kind of driver's license you will need if you are going to be driving a box truck, a school bus, a city bus, or any kind of large vehicle that is not a full-sized semi-truck and one that is under that weight category of 26,001 pounds.

Monetary Costs

As you can imagine, all of these licenses, permits, and registration processes will come with their own costs. Some costs can be categorized as fixed costs for the trucking business, while others are variable costs. The fixed costs will include the investment required for the vehicle, annual renewals of permits, annual taxes, regular maintenance expenses, and fixed insurance costs. In terms of the variable costs, the highest cost is fuel. You also need to factor in fines, unexpected costs, accidents and emergencies, and salaries you pay to drivers and other staff. In most cases, the variable costs will be higher than the fixed costs, and the fuel costs alone can account for 40%-45% of all operational costs.

Permit Charges

Some permits are issued once and have no renewal, such as the USDOT number. This is a one-time expense that will usually cost around $300.

The next main cost is the business registration cost, which will vary quite a lot from state to state and depend on the size and scope of the business. On average, you can safely assume that this cost will be between $200 and $500.

Then you have the Unified Carrier Registration (UCR), which may or may not be applicable for your locality. This is $69 for two vehicles or fewer and $206 for three to five vehicles.

Software Costs

If you are buying off-the-shelf solutions that will be installed on your machines in the office, you are looking at a one-time cost. For instance, if you are looking to buy accounting software that will be installed in-house, and you are the person managing that software, you only need to worry about the initial cost, which may be as little as $100. There will be no operational cost as you are using the software yourself. If you plan to hire an accountant, this will be a variable cost that you must factor in. One solution is to have the entire role of accounting outsourced; you won't have to worry about maintaining your own software, and you don't need to have an employee on-site. You will simply forward your information to the remote accountant, and they will compile this information for you. If you choose to go for a SaaS (Software as a Service) solution in which you use the software on a membership basis, you will have a monthly membership that you will pay or a fixed annual rent for the software. You can get a lot of solutions on the SaaS model. The main advantage is that you have constant support, security updates, and more reliability and security than a standalone system.

Other than that, you can get various management software that will help you do everything from admin support to payroll management to hiring new staff and managing existing payroll members.

As a trucking business, you aim to use as much technology as you can to your benefit, and one of the best investments you can make is a Transport Management System.

Transport Management System (TMS)

This is a lightly heavy investment for the business, but it is well worth the money in the operational advantages that it will give you. You can find complete TMS solutions that will cost around $5,000 to $10,000, while very high-end solutions can cost anywhere from $200,000 to $300,000. It all depends on the kind of functionality you are looking for, how big a fleet you want to manage, and whether or not you will be troubleshooting on your own or you will need tech assistance. A great solution is to look into what you really need for your business and then work your way backward. For instance, if you are only operating in a few states on the East coast, you don't need something that will give you national coverage. Similarly, if you do not want to get a full-sized solution, you can buy a smaller version of that, which gives you the functionality you need right now, and as you scale up, you can purchase more parts of the software and expand your abilities.

A TMS is a fantastic tool to help you optimize your routes, save money on fuel, improve driver performance, and even improve the safety and security of your vehicles. There are different TMS solutions available to choose from. Some require specialized hardware, whereas others can easily connect to readily available dashcams and other devices. Be sure to look around to see what meets your needs, but this is a bit of software that you definitely want to have in your business.

Insurance Costs

Insurance is a critical aspect of the trucking business, not only for the safety of the cargo but the safety of the vehicle, the business, and the employees. Not having the right kind of insurance for your vehicles and your business can be a serious problem. However, this will vary depending on various factors and can be a significant expense for the business. When it comes to insuring your vehicles and your equipment, the age of the machinery is essential. At the same time, the insurer will look at the kinds of materials that you transport, the regions within which you operate, and where your "yard" or home base is located.

Overall, you can expect the insurance for a full-size truck to be anywhere between $5,000 and $10,000 per year. However, this will depend on various factors such as the make and model of the vehicle, the vehicle's current condition, the driver's experience, and the safety systems installed in the vehicle. Determining the kind of coverage you need for your vehicle can be challenging, even though you can be sure that the older the vehicle, the lesser the premium will be. The newer the truck and the better its condition, the higher the premium you can expect.

Chapter 8: Can I Work from Home?

This question has come up several times recently, especially since COVID-19 has forced many businesses to consider working virtually. Many employers were reluctant to try this experiment at first and wouldn't have even considered it if the pandemic hadn't forced them to. The reason behind their reluctance is that they believe that employees won't be as productive at home, and it won't be easy to manage or monitor their performance. However, employers are starting to see the advantages of working from home and how it is a big and positive step for both employees and businesses. Employees who work from home are happier because they can strike a work-life balance, which can be hard to achieve if you work in an office. Happy employees are also more productive since they work in a comfortable environment. This productivity will naturally reflect on your business, and you will be able to reap its benefits.

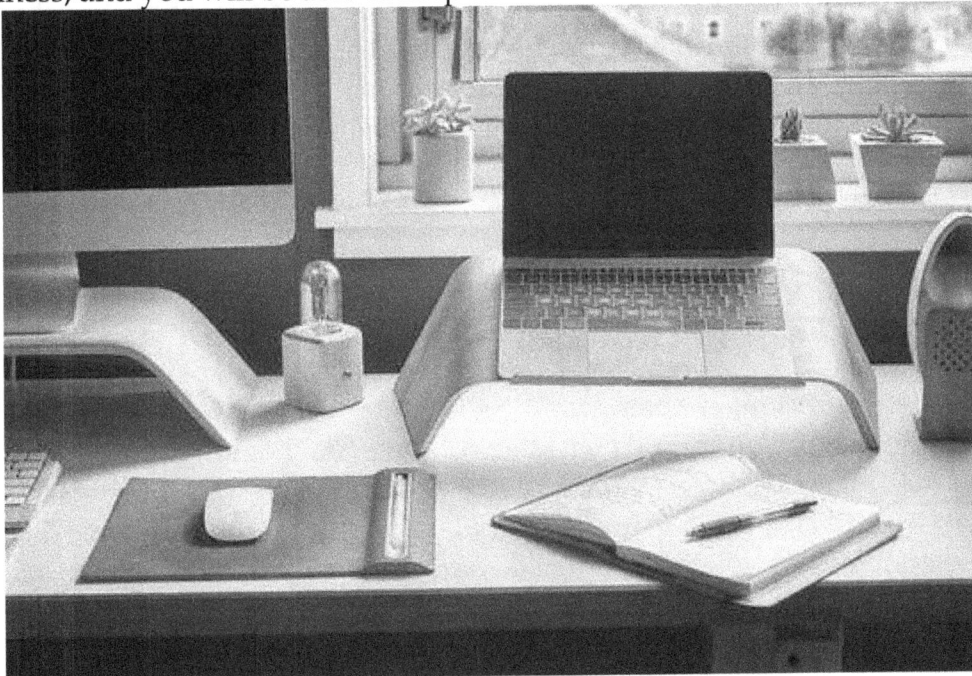

Another thing that employers worry about is that they may not be able to monitor or reach their employees as easily as when they are in the office. However, thanks to the many chatting apps available to us right now, they can easily connect with their team. Apps like Slack, Zoom, and Trello have made it easy for employers to have regular meetings with their employees, chat, and monitor their progress. Simply put, technology has made working from home a lot easier for both employees and employers.

Starting a freight brokerage business from home is a brilliant and cost-saving idea. This step will allow you to hire people from all over the world with different expertise and backgrounds to work remotely for you. Additionally, you will be able to save money on office rent, supplies, snacks, and electronic devices. Allowing your employees to work from home will give your business a good reputation for being a place that cares about their people's comfort and will make them loyal and less likely to quit.

If you are considering starting your freight business from home, now is a perfect time. Our lives have changed forever because of COVID-19. Now, we wear masks and practice social distancing to protect our lives. With new variants of the virus coming out every day, we can't be sure of what will happen next or if the governments will impose new restrictions and another lockdown. In this case, brick-and-mortar companies will have to shut down again. It is better to take this step now on your own terms while you are well-prepared for it instead of having to rush through things. If you are wondering if working from home is a good choice for your freight business or not, we are here to tell you that it is possible to run a freight business from home. That being said, you need to have the required knowledge and discipline while creating a space that can help you stay focused to succeed in this step. It would be best if you had a plan and a full understanding of running a business from home. If you are well-prepared, you will be able to take this step.

How to Run a Freight Brokerage Business from Home?

As mentioned in a previous chapter, starting a freight brokerage business is costly. If you are just starting, maybe you should consider working from home first. It will save you money and make it easier to start your business. Additionally, some people who worked in the logistics and transportation industry got laid off during the pandemic. If you are one of these people, then you have a huge advantage since you already have enough experience and knowledge to get you started. Whether you have the required background and knowledge or not, you can still take this step and work from home; you just need to know where to start first. Before we move forward, we need to stress that although running a freight brokerage business from home is possible, it isn't so simple. This isn't meant to discourage you. On the contrary, it's meant to emphasize the importance of being prepared to succeed in business.

Get the Required Knowledge and Training

As we have mentioned, if you have the required knowledge and experience, this will give you a huge advantage in starting your business. However, if you don't, you can learn. That being said, you can't learn about a business by researching it on Google. You need to have the necessary experience and knowledge about the shipping industry. There are two ways to do this. You can take a training course to learn how the freight industry works, or you can easily find many training courses online that will familiarize you with the industry and give you an idea of how to run and manage your business. If you aren't a fan of online education, you can take classes in your local college. Whatever method of learning you choose, stay updated on knowledge of the transportation business and state laws so you can perform your job without any issues.

Another way to help you gain expertise is by working part-time in shipping at any sort of business, even a department store. This may not seem like an ideal job for someone who wants to run their own business, but it can be an investment in your future as a freight broker. A part-time job will allow you to see how the business works, learn from the professionals, and observe how management handles any issues that can arise when running a freight business. It will also give you an idea of how shipping schedules and maintaining orders are handled.

You may need to educate yourself in certain areas like math because numbers play a huge role in a brokerage business. You will need strong communication skills, as you will spend most of your time networking, negotiating, and closing contracts. Technology is another thing that you will need to master. Since you will be running your business from home, you will be spending your working hours on your computer. However, we don't mean that you need to learn the basics like creating a spreadsheet or sending emails, with which most people are already familiar. You will have to learn more technical stuff because you won't be working in an office where an IT person will come to your aid if anything goes wrong. You may need to take a course or ask a friend who works in IT to explain what you need to do should any technical issues arise. Remember, you are running a business alone on your laptop or PC, and any glitches can affect your business.

Prepare a Budget

As we have mentioned, starting a business at home won't cost you as much as an office. That being said, you still need to prepare a budget for your home business. You will have to buy various equipment like smartphones, laptops, printers, copy machines, and fax machines. In addition to that, you will also need an internet connection, a phone landline, and office supplies. As a freight broker, you will also need specific software to help you manage your freight loads and customers. In addition to that, you should set money aside to pay for your license fees and register your business. Preparing a budget early on will make it easy to run your business efficiently and smoothly.

Get a License

One of the most important steps to start your freight brokerage home business is to acquire a license. To work as a freight broker in the USA, you will need to acquire a motor carrier authority from the FMCSA. This will enable you to work legally in the country. However, you should know that acquiring this license requires some time, so you should apply for it first.

Find Customers

After getting the necessary training, preparing a budget, and acquiring a license, you are all set to start your freight brokerage business from home. Since you are now in business, the first thing that you should do is to find customers. You can do this on your computer by searching on load boards for truckers to transport your goods. These boards will be beneficial if you are just starting and don't have many connections yet. That being said, you should ensure you work with trusted truckers since your reputation will depend on it. So go online and do some research to get started. You will find many load boards online; some are free, while others require a fee.

Separate Your Finances

You need to separate your business and personal finances, and the best way to do that is by setting up a business bank account. If you don't have separate bank accounts, you may spend your personal money on your business or vice versa, affecting your finances and business budget. Keeping your finances separated will help you keep track of your expenses and avoid any financial problems.

Create a Home Office

One of the main problems that people who work from the home face is distractions. If you have kids or live with family members or roommates, you may not be able to focus on your work easily. Whether it is television noise or your kids playing and screaming, these factors can make you struggle to stay focused. Freight brokerage business requires networking either by talking on the phone or chatting online, so you need to block out any external noises. Additionally, our homes are where we relax and kick back, so working in bed or on a couch may negatively impact our productivity. Therefore, you will need to set up a home office in a quiet spot at your home. If you don't have an empty room, you can work in your garage or set up a spot in any of your rooms for work. To avoid distractions and have privacy, make sure the space you create has a door. Additionally, it should have a professional atmosphere, so you won't feel the need to kick back or fall asleep. It simply needs to have a chair and desk so you can be focused and alert.

Set a Schedule and Stick to It

Working from home gives you the chance to set your own schedule. You can work at night or in the day, or at any hours you want. You are your own boss. That being said, you shouldn't work for over eight hours. Some people who work from home fail to strike the home-life balance. Since they are always at the place where they work, they seem to be always working, and their personal life and mental health suffer as a result. Therefore, you will need to set a schedule, stick to it, and avoid working after hours. Remember that you are starting and running your own business. If you burn out, you won't be able to keep going, which can negatively impact your new business. After you finish work, turn off your computer and your business phone, and relax.

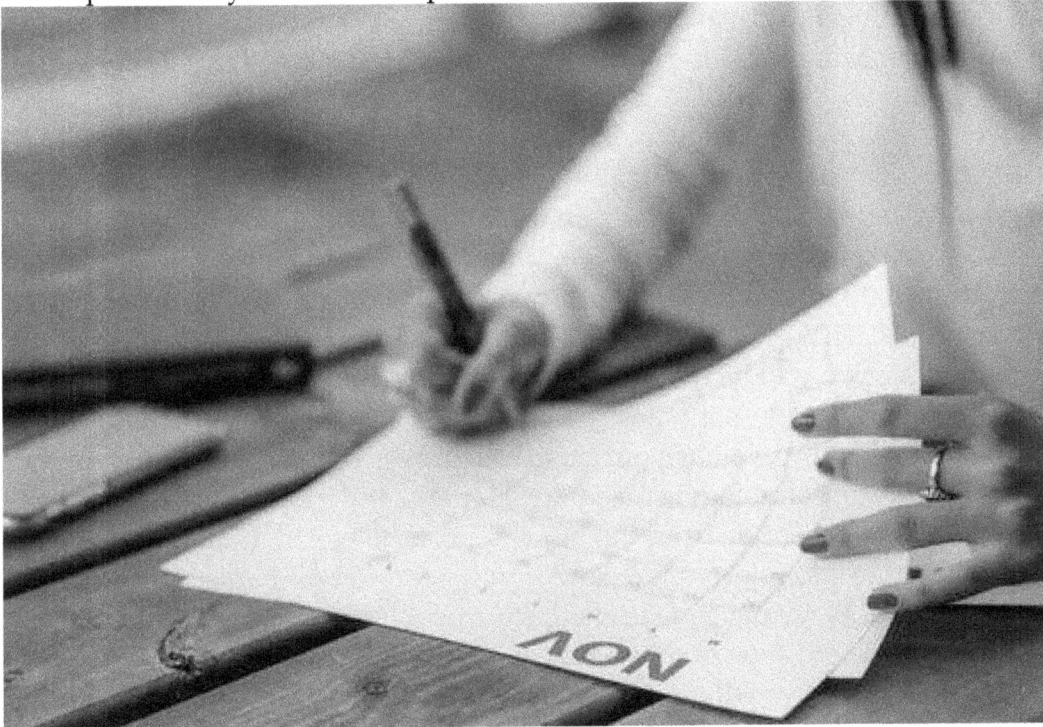

On the other hand, a downside to working from home is that being your own boss means taking breaks whenever you want and for as long as you want. This can negatively affect your productivity and your workflow. You don't want to have a reputation as someone who slacks off or isn't focused on their work. There is no denying that you will need a break. Just treat yourself like you are in an office and take a one-hour break at a fixed time every day. Simply put, set a schedule, and stick to it.

Hire an Accountant

Starting a business from home means that you won't have a team around you to help you manage important things like finances. So, you will need to hire an accountant to help you manage your finances. Naturally, you will make money running your freight brokerage business. You will also spend money, which is normal for any business. An accountant will manage your finances and keep you aware of your profits and expenses. If your expenses are bigger than your profits, this will mean that your business is losing money or isn't profitable. An accountant will help you keep track of your expenses to see if there is a way to save money.

Additionally, you will also have to pay taxes. To avoid any confusion with filing your taxes, an accountant can take care of this for you and will keep you updated with any new tax laws. That being said, one of the advantages of working from home is that it will allow you to claim tax deductions for utilities, insurance, and rent.

Whether working from home will be our new norm or not is up in the air. That being said, as a result of the uncertainties that we live in right now, it seems like it is the safest bet. However, working from home isn't an option for every career. For instance, neither doctors nor nurses can afford this luxury. On the other hand, being a freight broker is one of the jobs one can do from home. You just need the right experience, equipment, and papers to get you started.

Additionally, since you will be working from home by yourself, you need to educate yourself in various areas like software and communication skills to efficiently run your business by yourself. However, as your business grows, you will need to hire other employees. Thanks to technology, you can reach them and monitor their progress easily online. Even if you hire people from the other side of the world, managing them won't be a problem. Every business starts small, and if you want to build an empire, you will need to start somewhere. As we have mentioned, starting a business from home will cost you much less than having to run your business at an office. It makes sense if you are still starting to find options that will help you save money since you will need every penny at this early stage of the business until you build your clientele. You can still grow and have a successful business even if you work from home. You just need to develop the right plan and strategies to get you started.

Chapter 9: Scaling Your Business

Scaling is critical in the operations of any business since it promotes growth. However, it is not very easy to scale a business, but the good thing is that you can consider different methods for this activity. Thus, this chapter explains what scaling is and why it is important in business. The next section discusses digital marketing, followed by a detailed explanation of SMART business strategy and how it can help you scale your venture. The final part focuses on the importance of specializing in a specific niche in your business and how it can help you gain traction.

What Is Scaling?

When you decide to grow your business, you can consider the option of scaling. Even if you manage to sell many things, you should be able to deliver to the clients. Scalability is mainly concerned with capability and capacity. You need to check if your business can grow or if the employees and infrastructure can accommodate the growth. If your company's growth fails to suit the clients' needs, you will likely have unhappy consumers. This will not be good for your venture. This is why you need to consider scaling.

Scaling is a process that allows business owners to set the stage to support the growth of their companies. It means you have the ability and what is required to grow without being hampered. All you need is planning, staff, the right systems, processes, some funding, partners, and technology. With scaling, you can increase your revenue without increasing resources. The processes you can scale are the ones you can do in bulk without any extra effort. For instance, email marketing allows you to instantly send a single email to more than one million people. You do not need extra staff to perform the same task even if you have increased your number of customers.

Scaling your business is more than growth; it is the capability to handle the increasing input. If you fail to deliver your products or services to the customers, growth can negatively impact your operations. To scale means you can cost-effectively handle the increased workload to meet the customers' demands without overstretching your capability. When every business starts, the owners look at scalability, and you can achieve this by looking at your plan, marketing, and sales strategies. You can use scaling as a test to see whether your plan is achievable or not.

You should consider scaling your business for several reasons since all operators aim to grow at some point. You should reach a break-even point where you recover your costs and start making profits from your operations. The main thing you should know about scaling your business is increasing revenue without incurring huge costs. When you add revenue and customers, the costs should not be much, if any. Your business stands high chances of survival if it is ready to grow and accommodate the changes that come with growth. It can also enjoy longevity and durability to remain on the right path.

Scaling your business helps improve its efficiency since you plan for any eventuality. This means that you are prepared to operate in different circumstances when you decide to grow your venture. The other plus is that you can enjoy consistency in your operations. When you scale your business, you are committed to succeeding under different conditions.

Scaling also helps you maintain flexibility to adapt to different pressures and economic changes. All you need to do is to know when you should up-scale or down-scale to suit the needs of your business. If you carefully consider scalability, your business can survive long into the future. You will also become a strong competitor in the industry if you successfully scale your venture.

Another essential aspect you should know about scaling is that it isn't just about expanding your business. You may need to scale down your operations to meet reduced demands in some instances. This could result from natural cycles in the industry, which may be out of your control. Issues like recessions or fundamental changes in the industry can break your business, so you must be prepared for anything that can happen.

Scalability is also concerned with knowing when to change tack and ensuring you have the appropriate resources. If you are not prepared to scale, then it is just as good as planning to fail. When you experience an economic boom, make sure you can meet the demands, and your employees must be able to adapt to the changes to deliver quality service. You need a cash flow plan that can help you meet all the changes in the environment in which you operate. If you encounter a sudden downturn in your operations, you must have a plan in place to help you cut costs. It would be best if you also streamlined your operations to continue to run efficiently even under pressure.

The Importance of Digital Marketing

Digital marketing is a valuable tool that can go a long way in promoting the growth of your business, and it also helps you build authoritative online visibility. In this digital age, online presence is critical for the survival of your business, and many marketers believe that different marketing strategies like search engine optimization, email marketing, and pay-per-click (PPC) advertising are successful in raising brand awareness. If you invest in digital marketing, you are likely to experience steady growth in your business.

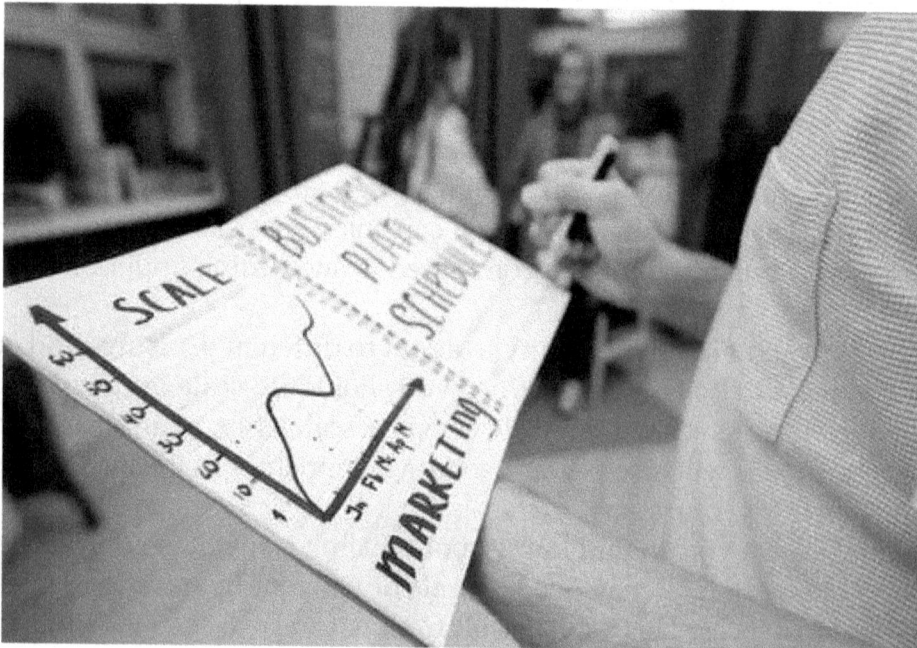

Email marketing is an effective strategy you can consider scaling in your business since it does not require a substantial increase in resources. With this strategy, you can automate your communication to improve efficiency. Email marketing helps you reach several people, a hundred people, or thousands of people instantly without additional labor to perform the task. You can also personalize your emails to appeal to the emotional interests of individual customers. According to various research, there are higher chances that the recipient will read and respond to an email addressed to their name. This can help you expand your customer base, which is good for your business.

The other benefit of investing in technology is that it makes it cheaper and easier to scale a business. You can enjoy large economies of scale with less labor. Automation helps reduce manual work, lowers cost, and improves efficiency. Systems integration is a critical area you should improve in your operations to promote cohesion among different departments.

Target Appropriate Audience

Digital marketing helps you target the ideal audience to avoid wasting time and resources dealing with people who may not fit into your operations. If you deal directly with the right consumers, you can get the leads that can help improve your sales. With this strategy, you can target the ideal audience more precisely and tailor your messages to suit your needs. You can include the information you want to shape your marketing campaigns to appeal to the interests of the target audience.

Improve Competition

When you are in business, you should know that you are operating in an environment with competitors, and they also use digital marketing in their operations. You can only gain a competitive advantage if you use similar tools your competitors utilize to market their products and services. Another benefit of using technology is that it helps you research the market to learn how your competitors operate. It also helps improve different functions of your business, like sales management, CRM, marketing automation, manufacturing, and accounting. With the right system, you can significantly improve efficiency in your operations.

Technology Helps You Locate People

You can use new technology such as social media to reach people where they spend most of their time. Many people spend most of their time online, and they use the internet to perform various tasks in life. The internet is now an integral part of our everyday life since we use it to conduct searches, shop online, and check social media. Most customers are always online, which helps you reach them by identifying the channels they commonly use.

Many customers use the internet to look for different products and services they need before buying them. Therefore, you must use the search engine optimization strategy to improve the ranking of your website on search engine results pages. SEO is based on the keyword's relevance and quality content you provide to different users. You have to optimize your pages since you cannot buy your way to the top of the search engine results pages. Similarly, make sure your advertising is relevant when using the PPC (Pay per Click) strategy. Google usually ranks different types of advertisements based on their relevance.

Therefore, when you use SEO, make sure you provide consistent and quality content that can help improve your site's ranking. Try to create relevant content with unique keywords that make your brand stand out from the rest. With digital marketing, you can get the opportunity to compete with large companies to generate more leads.

Quality Customer Service

Digital marketing can go a long way in helping you provide quality customer service to your clients. Many customers are primarily interested in the quality of service they get from a company, and only then do they develop loyalty. Happy customers are likely to come for repeat business, which can help you scale your operations. You can use different social media platforms to engage with your clients or remind them about your business. When you respond to customers' needs, it shows that you respect them, and they can positively respond to your market offerings. The other important thing is to conduct periodic market research to understand the buyers' needs.

Track Your Campaigns

Digital marketing is vital for your business because it helps you monitor and track your campaigns. If you are promoting a product or service, you can use a marketing or advertising campaign. When you invest money and time in the campaign, you need to know if it is working. It becomes easy to track the campaign and make better decisions with digital marketing. For instance, you can assess the response rate to your campaign. This will help you make necessary changes to attract many potential buyers.

SMART Business Strategy

A SMART business strategy involves creative and innovative ideas you can use to solve problems in your operations. This plan must be based on specific, measurable, achievable, relevant, and time-bound (SMART) goals. During hard economic times, the best managers know that they must think outside the box and avoid decisions that can compromise the company's future financial situation. This is the main reason why you should design a SMART business plan.

When you use SMART principles in your business, your goals are *specific* and *measurable*. It would be best to avoid vague goals or believe that everyone can be a potential customer. Instead, you must specify the exact client you want to deal with in your business plan. This will help you focus on the target clients' needs to provide the best services. Remember that your goals must be measurable, given that there is competition in the freight industry.

It is essential to set *achievable* goals to remain focused on your business. Many people fail to achieve their goals because they are overambitious or want to achieve great things within a very short space. Unfortunately, this may not be possible when you are in business. You need to work with *relevant* and *time-bound* objectives to not lose track of your business.

Once you have your SMART business plan, you must communicate it to the team members to understand what is expected of them. You can use your plan to enhance elements like creativity in the organization. Downsizing is not the best thing to consider when facing challenges in your operations. If your business is booming, you have to be smart enough to avoid rushing into hiring new employees. This is not the essence of scaling your venture, which emphasizes maximizing revenue while maintaining expenses at the minimum level.

If your business is not performing well, you can consider scaling down and taking drastic measures that can help you lower expenses. For instance, you can offer full-time employees unpaid vacations or cut overtime and bonus payments until things normalize again. Laying off workers is not a good thing since you may never get them back. You also need to look at your travel and supply expenses to see where you can save some money.

Another effective strategy to boost your profits is to engage community members and create a buzz about your service to appeal to the interests of many people. You must get some people to talk to friends or family about their experiences with your service. You also need to use social media posts to build your profile to attract more customers. Buzz marketing can involve contests or promotions where your company gives away some prices to lucky winners. These activities help you engage with the community, and you can also give the proceeds to charity.

While you may need money to make more money, it is possible to scale your business without spending any money. With a SMART business strategy, you can cut excess spending and stop things like rapid expansion. You can also seek lower marketing rates and focus on improving your core product or service to attract more consumers.

Significance of Focusing on a Specific Niche

When you are a freight broker business, it is good to focus on a specific niche to gain traction and positively impact your business. A niche is a targetable and focused segment of the market you can serve. When you decide to concentrate on niche markets, you become a specialist who provides a service or product that mainly focuses on clients' specific needs – something that dominant providers in the industry don't cover well, if at all.

As you are now aware, the freight industry is quite big, involving many divisions. You can scale your business by identifying an unmet need and analyzing the gaps that exist in the market. For instance, you can focus on removals or transportation of fresh produce where you commit yourself to excellent services that will suit the target audience's needs. Niche marketing allows you to focus on a specific group of people instead of believing that everyone is your potential customer. The challenge is that you may not be able to serve everyone, so it is vital to focus on what you can do best.

Advantages of Finding a Niche

You can get many advantages from finding a niche, especially if your business is still small and you want to scale it up. This strategy can help you build a loyal audience, thereby creating a steady revenue stream. A particular group of buyers will always want to buy from you instead of competitors if they are happy about your services. You should constantly do market research to understand the beliefs and attitudes that influence the buying behavior of your target consumers.

The niche marketing strategy helps you identify and target your potential customers since the pool of people belonging to a niche is usually smaller than mainstream markets. You can easily become an expert in your area of specialization, and many people will know what you do. Clients will also identify with your business if you position it well in the market. A niche is generally smaller in size, which means you can quickly become well known by the people interested in the services you offer.

Your profile and visibility will improve within this group, and this will help you attract more referrals. You can easily scale up your business through referrals since you do not need to invest any money in marketing-related activities like advertising. Satisfied customers can easily refer high-quality clients to your business. This will help you generate more revenue from your operations as you expand your customer base.

If your business model is unique, you will likely face less competition. The main advantage is that you will be providing specific products and services for specific people. In short, this means that you already have your clients, and your competition cannot easily copy your strategy. This makes marketing much easier as you can easily attract the right people without wasting a lot of money on activities like advertising.

People who share the same interests tend to behave similarly and are also attracted by similar things. Your clients will do the marketing job for you since they will refer interested clients to your company. More importantly, you will also enjoy repeat business from happy clients. Consumers will come back for more, which promotes the growth of your relationship.

Once you establish a business, the next thing you should focus on is its scalability, which must be the key consideration for your marketing plan. When you scale your venture, you can increase the revenue you generate without spending a lot of money. Scaling your business is concerned with finding the right balance to help your business adjust to the ups and downs of operations. It helps you know when to respond to the changing demands of your company.

Chapter 10: Staffing, Money Management and Crises

Being a freight broker has its fair share of challenges, and you cannot escape that. When stepping into this business, you are expected to be arranging efficient transportation services between various freight companies in need of this service. But what you may not have expected is the amount of help you will soon need. Because as soon as the business grows, you will need to hire more people to help with the business responsibilities.

Once you hire new people, there are different aspects you need to consider about managing them, and there are certain crises that may arise. This chapter will discuss hiring new staff and what you should be doing if you need more people on the team, the best management strategies for a freight brokerage business, and how to handle a crisis in the best possible manner.

What Happens If I Need Staff?

Hiring new people may seem overwhelming (especially for a startup business owner). Nevertheless, it is necessary because you cannot hope to make your business successful and efficient without this. If you try to manage everything all by yourself or with limited staff, you would not be able to maintain high-quality customer service, and neither would you be able to attend to details. In addition to the drop in service quality, you will have to refuse many more projects because of the work overload. You may also risk losing the existing customer base because of the service quality or inability to meet the timelines. The solution is quite simple: outsource responsibilities by hiring efficient, professional team members.

I will not coax you with false hope. Hiring new members and expanding your business is downright terrifying for any business owner! But it is something that you have to do if you dream of dominating the market or simply adding more value to your business. To alleviate being overwhelmed by this situation and face the fear of expanding your business, you may need to consider a few things:

1. What Is Your Why?

This may sound redundant to your ears, but it's not. It is the most important thing you have to do as a freight broker business owner. Once you identify the reason behind hiring new people, it will feel less overwhelming, and you will be able to appreciate and focus on the benefits it will bring. This may simply mean that you see the need to hire a person to handle dispatch, get more leads, or perhaps explore another niche. This will help you stay focused and refrain from confusing your staff members about their job roles. It is recommended to avoid putting all responsibilities on a person or mixing up the job roles (unless you have pre-planned this and wanted this). Adding too many responsibilities or unrelated tasks to a new hire's workload may overwhelm your worker, and you may risk losing them.

2. Hire Smartly!

Generally, business owners and HR managers prefer resumes with years of experience. But you have to understand that experience does not guarantee skills and analytical insight. You may find yourself caught up in a tug-of-war between hiring an experienced professional or a newbie.

Both have pros and cons; when you hire someone new, you can save a lot on your budget and hire more people for the money you have. You can also train the newbie according to your company's unique environment, so they understand your work process better. You can hire a newbie and train them enough to get them up to speed, but you cannot expect them to display the innate skills, attitudes, and analytical insight of a seasoned professional.

On the other hand, you can hire an experienced and seasoned worker and save a lot of training time. Hiring one skilled employee is way better than hiring four inexperienced ones. Whoever you end up hiring, it is important that they understand your company culture and can fit into it comfortably. So, figure out smart ways to put your workers' analytical and critical thinking to the test. You cannot hope to grow your business by just increasing the headcount; it will take a lot more than that.

3. Do You Really Have Tasks for Them?

Nobody else knows about this! It is your business, and you are the best person to carefully evaluate whether you have enough work for the new team member or not. If you are in the freight business and your business is growing, you should know that the most required team member is always the dispatcher. Hiring dispatchers will take a lot of burden off your plate because they will be helping you dispatch drivers, cover loads, call check-ins, and scheduling. This will free enough time for you to focus on other aspects of the business, such as customer support.

4. Keep Your Business Flexible

You cannot decide to hire a bunch of workers after merely a terrible day at work because it will take a lot more than that. Even a month or two will not justify this because even the most efficient teams face hard times occasionally and struggle with work management, but this does not mean hiring a dozen new members will solve the problem. To step towards hiring staff members, you have to ask yourself whether you have enough work for the new members or not. Imagine what it would be like with the new team members in the slowest seasons of your business.

5. Double-Check Your Budget

When you are about to hire new staff, you must have enough budget to accommodate the intake. It does not make any sense to add more people to the team without having the budget to support them. So, carefully consider your budget before expanding your team and business. Often, freight broker startup owners misunderstand the concept of budget evaluation while hiring staff members. It is easy to think that budget would only mean the staff salaries, but it is more than that. You cannot hope to bring new people to your team and not have enough equipment for them to work with (this may include printers, desks, computers, chairs, headsets, or other necessary supplies). You may also require a bigger office with more staff members in the team.

Lastly, when you add more people to your team, you are actually growing your business, which means adding more power to your business. This adds to your responsibility as a business owner because you will have to manage your team effectively. As a team leader, you will have to lead by example and be patient with your team. It is also essential to give the team ample opportunities to learn and grow while monitoring their progress closely.

How Can I Manage My Company's Money Efficiently?

When hiring your staff, the budget is one of the most important factors to consider. You cannot turn a blind eye to your budget and assume that everything will float fine. Efficiently managing your company's money should be your top priority. Handling cash flow effectively is one of a business owner's biggest and most common struggles.

Money management does not have to be a nightmare, but you do need to have a sound management strategy in place to handle it effectively. This will enable you to overcome any negative cash flow periods and keep your business on a profitable track. We will discuss five effective strategies to manage your freight broker business's cash flow or money without any hiccups.

1. Keep an Eye on the Expenses

As a business owner, you must be well aware of the expenses in your business on a daily, weekly, monthly, and yearly basis. If you are not keeping a close eye on the expenses, things are bound to go out of hand pretty fast, and you won't even realize it when this happens. It is quite common for businesses to have several accounts, such as savings, checking, or credit card accounts, and keeping them maintained and monitored is very important. Without proper management of finances, misuse of funds or overspending can easily happen. So, ensure that you have a detailed record of all the accounts and closely monitor the withdrawals.

2. Keep Personal and Business Expenses Separate

It is easy to mix things up and fall prey to this account fiasco when you are just starting as a freight broker and have a small business at hand. It is highly recommended to keep your business account absolutely separate from your personal account, no matter what. This stands true even if you are not required to keep two different accounts. Mixing your business and personal funds will create absolute chaos and disorganization, and you will not be able to track the profitability accurately and efficiently.

3. Create a Smart Budget and Stick to It

This is non-negotiable. Without a clearly defined budget for your small business expenses, you are highly prone to indulging in *unnecessary expenses*. Therefore, it is advisable to create a functional budget for different business categories. When you are aware of the limit to spend for a particular category, you will most likely stay in that budgeted amount. Your budget will also help you forecast the revenue you will receive as a business. If your expected revenue is less than the budgeted amount, then you will minimize the expenditure or think of ways to increase income streams.

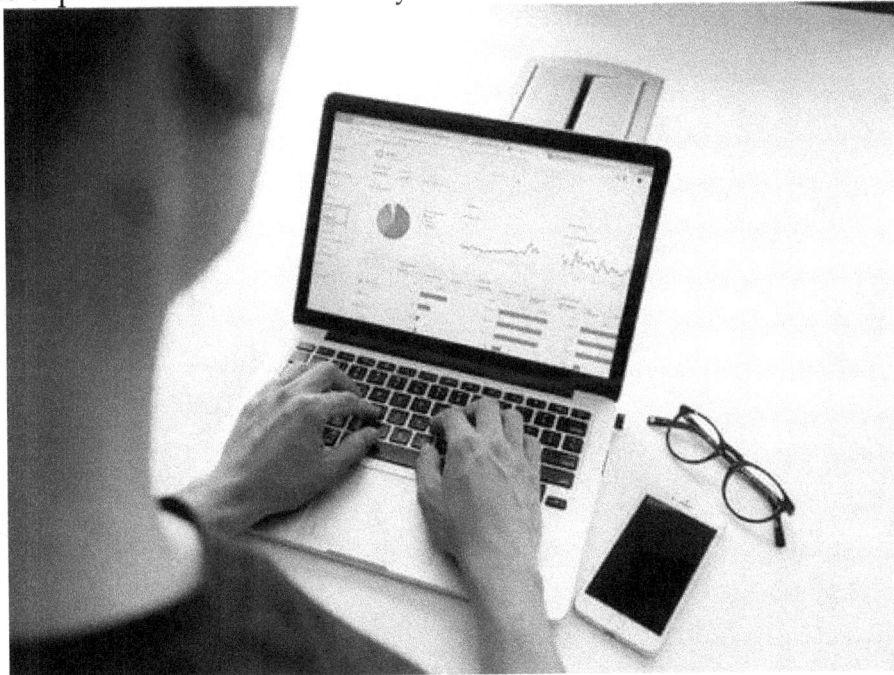

4. Optimize Revenue and Cut Down Expense

This is a very straightforward strategy for managing money in your freight business, but it can be tricky to accomplish. All you have to do is to minimize expenses and increase income! But it's easier said than done. As a business, if you need to minimize the expenses, the first thing to do is to analyze the expenses, which will help you scale down and eliminate unnecessary expenses. Moreover, you can brainstorm ways to increase the revenue. This may mean offering discounts, promoting additional services, or rigorously marketing.

5. Have Cash in Reserve

This will save you a lot of mental fatigue and time worrying about an unexpected cash crunch. In the freight business, there will be times when you will run into unexpected situations or crises, and at that time, your reserved cash will save you a lot of trouble. So, keep some extra revenue reserved for times like these.

Should I Hire an Accountant?

While hiring an accountant for a freight broker is not compulsory, it's an expense you won't regret. At first, you may think it is unreasonable to hire an accountant when it seems there's no need. In reality, it is good and can help you save some money. Hiring an accountant for a freight agent is always a wise decision for several reasons.

A professional accountant has the knowledge and understanding of the tax laws. When you hire one, they make sure to claim all the deductions for your business. Moreover, they also check and file your tax forms correctly. The chance of error gets reduced.

Being a 1099 freight agent means there's no withholding tax. You pay taxes on whatever income you earn as a freight broker. The state and federal taxes may differ. But when you have a local tax accountant in your team, they know the state and federal tax laws. The accountant will ensure that your business is not overpaying or underpaying the taxes.

Hiring an accountant isn't just limited to tax filing. You can also use their knowledge for other financial matters. Many things can impact your taxes during the business, like leasing an office space, hiring more employees, or buying a house. While you may not predict those changes, an accountant can enable your business to be well prepared for such changes. They can advise you so you can make the best-informed decisions. The most important reason a freight broker needs an accountant is to save time. When you hire an accountant, not only do you save money, but it also frees up your time. It may take several hours or even days for a freight broker to complete their tax filing. In contrast, when a freight broker outsources this task to a professional accountant, they can save all that time. In short, hiring an accountant for a freight business means investing that time and money in your business.

What to Do If Something Goes Wrong

Just like any other business, as a freight broker, you may run into several crises that make you feel cornered. The critical thing to remember in such situations is to keep moving forward and understand that you are not alone in this situation. Challenges are part of any successful business journey, and you get to learn so much from them. However, if you are aware of the possible issues or problematic situations beforehand, you can be better prepared to handle them. This will help you better manage everything and prevent you from feeling overwhelmed. We will discuss the four most commonly reported issues freight brokers face and a few ideas on how to handle them in the best possible manner.

1. When Communication Is Off the Mark

Communication plays a vital role in keeping a business functional, and it is critical for the long-term success of a company. Freight brokerage is a demanding business and requires your team to stay ahead of the work process, which also means maintaining a clear line of communication. A lack of efficient and consistent communication will result in multiple errors, delays, and general dismay among team members. It will also make your customers highly dissatisfied with your company because a team that is struggling with effective communication will not be able to meet customer requirements appropriately. The solution to this problem is quite simple: maintain a clear line of communication. You can plan periodic team meetings to ensure that everyone is on the same page and have some way for team members to interact and build rapport so your staff is comfortable communicating with each other. Introducing communication skills workshops may also be a great initiative. You have to understand that communication should not be a burden, and for a team to be functional, the communication must be seamless.

2. Company Growth and Margin Pressure

The efficiency of any business is determined by how well it manages the margin pressure, that narrow space between profitability and loss. It requires knowledge and understanding of tight-capacity markets. Your relationships with customers, carriers, shippers, and receivers also play an important part. A good approach is to research the peak time or season of commodity production that your targeted customer is interested in. This will help you solve your customer's problem.

For carriers, instead of dial-a-truck, it's better to target those carriers that can offer capacity and execute at your customer's service-level agreement. It's best to pick the carriers with a home base near your shipper/receiver's location.

You should also be mindful of your shipper/receiver as they impact your sales margin. You can build a good relationship with your shipper/receiver with an ideal appointment time and load time within three hours or less.

3. The Carrier Base Is Everything!

For a freight brokerage business, its carrier base plays a vital role in increasing or decreasing the sales margin. You need to build the same rapport with your carriers as you have with your customers. You can easily maintain good relationships with your carrier by finding common ground since they are your extensions.

4. Is There a "Guaranteed" Capacity?

As a freight brokerage business, you do not really own a fleet of trucks. This means that it is hard to put an absolute number on the "capacity" of available vehicles. This can easily result in problems relating to following a schedule and may cause frustration for customers and team members. The solution to this problem is to set a time limit for pre-booking the service because, without this, you cannot manage the customer requests on time. To have a good reputation in the market, you need to maintain an impeccable record in keeping up with the schedule. Another important thing is to take responsibility if a deadline is missed and try to pair up with reliable carriers so that these issues remain a rare occurrence.

5. Finding the Right Talent and Nurturing It

This is more important than you may realize. The biggest obstacle you may face as a freight broker is having team members who are underperforming or under-qualified. The logistics and transportation industry is considered one of the most competitive markets. This means that if you are not doing everything to stay ahead of your competitors, you will get trampled on. To perform well, you need to have a team of skilled and well-qualified professionals who know their roles well. Successful business owners understand the significance of an efficient team and invest time and resources to find the right team members.

Now that you know what it takes to manage your freight broker business from the start, you will be better prepared to handle anything that comes along this journey. Knowing when you need a bigger team, how to manage the team and finances properly, and how to handle the most commonly occurring crises in a freight broker business will help you stay on top of everything. The most important thing is to keep trying because starting a business (any business) is all about learning as you go, improvising, and innovating. Every cautious step or calculated risk that you take should ultimately fuel the overall growth of your business.

Conclusion

The freight industry is easily one of the oldest forms of business on the planet, and it has a lot of potential in the future as the overall value of business rises. As we see more commerce taking place than ever before, there will be a higher need for services that complement commerce, and the transport of physical goods plays a pivotal role in this process. Wherever you are in the world, getting into the freight forwarding business in any role will be a good idea for the future.

If you are looking to get into a business with a low risk yet a very high earning potential, then being a freight broker might be the right choice. Freight brokers deal with very high-value investments, and even a single truck can carry several thousands of dollars worth of material. When you consider the example of freight forwarding companies that transport hazardous chemicals, fuel, and luxury items like super sports cars, this figure can easily cross the million-dollar mark.

Moreover, we now live in the digital era, in a time where setting up a business of any kind doesn't require you to go through a lot of paperwork or get into any kind of complex process. You can do nearly everything that you need to while being completely remote. Your employees can be virtual, your operations can be based on the cloud, and you can be anywhere in the world running a business that operates in every part of the world.

However, with all the advantages to being in business today, there are some challenges that you must watch for. Things like digital security, leveraging your digital assets, and keeping up with the fast pace of the modern economy are things that you want to watch out for. It is not surprising to see organizations that have been around for years and even decades go out of business today. In most cases, it is because they failed to keep up with changing consumer trends and an evolving economic situation.

This book highlights some critical things you need to keep in mind when planning your business, setting up shop, and things you need to continuously tweak once business commences. Even though you can do a lot of these things on your own, it would always be worth the money to have a professional help you out. Unlike in the past, where the bulk of the investment was in the business's infrastructure, you will spend more money on the human resource you employ today.

Everyone has access to nearly all the same resources. Whether it is the internet, devices, social media, or premade software solutions, the main difference lies in how effectively you use these solutions to your advantage.

Even today, the one thing that you will need is some kind of capital to get the ball rolling. You can look into several options to get financing for your business idea. However, make sure you weigh out the options and understand the long-term consequences of choosing a lender. You don't have to have something that will be cheap to start but turns out to be so expensive in the long run that it leaves you with no profitability.

Lastly, the power of personal relationships is still evident today. Whenever you are starting a business, you need to pay extra attention to your network and actively work towards improving the kind of and amount of people that you have access to.

As they say, it is not how much you know, but *who you know* that will determine your business success. You don't have to know everything, as long as you can get the right people to do what they're experts at.

www.ingramcontent.com/pod-product-compliance
Lightning Source LLC
Chambersburg PA
CBHW081825200326
41597CB00023B/4386